"We have had many straight biographies of writers in recent years . . . that leave their subjects curiously diminished. Mr. McConkey's achievement . . . is to send the reader back to the Russian master with renewed wonder."

—HARVEY SHAPIRO, *The New York Times*

"What a pleasure, and how much there is to learn from this short book!"

—DENISE LEVERTOV

"A deeply moving, exquisitely written book."

—JAY PARINI, *The Washington Post Book World*

"An important book, 'important' in the sense that it speaks to issues and interests well beyond those so adroitly addressed by the author."

—GEORGE GARRETT

"One of our finest writers."

—ANNIE DILLARD

Obelisk

TO A DISTANT ISLAND

ALSO BY JAMES McCONKEY

TO A DISTANT
ISLAND

James McConkey

A Dutton **O**belisk Paperback

E. P. DUTTON / NEW YORK

Published in the United States by E. P. Dutton,
a division of New American Library,
2 Park Avenue, New York, N.Y. 10016.

Library of Congress Catalog Number:
86-71256

ISBN: 0-525-48256-3

Published simultaneously in Canada by
Fitzhenry & Whiteside Limited, Toronto.

W

Designed by Mark O'Connor

10 9 8 7 6 5 4 3 2 1

CONTENTS

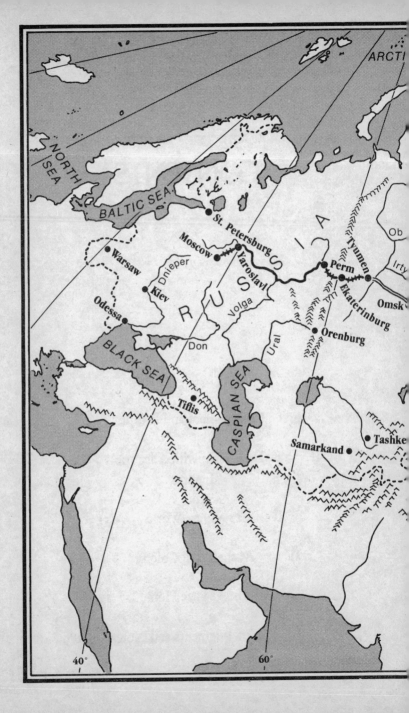

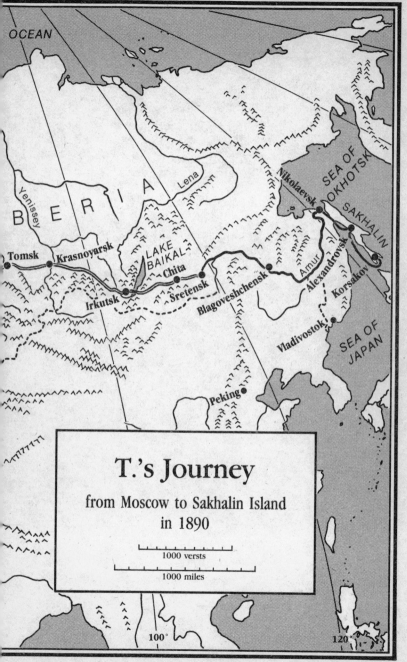

OCEAN

S I B E R I A

Yenissey

Lena

Tomsk   Krasnoyarsk

Irkutsk

LAKE BAIKAL

Chita

Sretensk

Blagoveshchensk

Amur

Alexandrovsk

Korsakov

Nikolaevsk

SEA OF OKHOTSK

SAKHALIN

Vladivostok

SEA OF JAPAN

Peking

T.'s Journey

from Moscow to Sakhalin Island
in 1890

1000 versts

1000 miles

100°

120°

Map by David Price

I

Confinement and
Escape

1

In late April of the year 1890, T., who had been undergoing a depression so severe that his most recent biographer believes he might have been nearing a breakdown, left his home in Moscow for the penal colony on the island of Sakhalin, a journey of over sixty-five hundred miles, or more than a quarter of our planet's circumference. Knowing little about the expanse he would be traversing without friends or previously-known companions, but imagining it could contain dangerous beasts and escaped convicts who were murderers, he purchased a knife ("useful also for salami," he said) and a revolver. His goal led him eastward over a vast land mass, and since his itinerary kept him generally a good distance north of the fiftieth parallel, he saw little that was green or hopeful. The rain and cold of the early portion of the trip, made by train and riverboat (there were ice floes on the Kama, the second of the rivers he sailed on), continued during the strenuous middle portion, a three-thousand mile ride in a series of horse-drawn carriages; he traveled through the mud of the spring thaw, sometimes through wide but shallow lakes made by the flooding of the rivers. He was fortunate to escape death from drowning or road accidents—once, indeed, he was thrown to the ground in a crash. The inns were as filthy as they were infrequent, and T. (although he had been coughing up blood at intervals for more than five years) adjusted fairly well to sleeping in his damp clothes on the straw bed of his *tarantass*, a four-wheeled chaise without seats or springs whose only protection against the weather was a canopy, as it jolted through the night from one post station to the next. In the final weeks of the journey, the clouds dispersed, and the brilliant sun abruptly brought the heat of summer; now the mud was replaced by a heavy dust, augmented by the smoke of forest fires, that clotted T.'s nose, irritated his eyes, and so covered his face and clothes that he seemed, even to himself, an apparition, the gray ghost of a beggar or of a murdered traveler, or even of one of the murderers he had armed himself against. Ultimately, he transferred back to the relative comfort of riverboats, and—upon reaching the shore of the continent—took a steamer to his island. There he stayed for three months, visiting the prisons and various settlements. He saw a flogging, or as much of it as he could bear, and suffered from a recurrent nightmare as a consequence. And he saw convicts at an extremity of degradation in which personality itself was gone, and speech as well; their appeals were those of sick or starving animals. For perhaps the first time in his life, he was visited with migraine headaches. With the cooperation of the authorities, he managed nevertheless to compile a census not only of the convicts, but of former convicts who were required to remain in exile and had been granted settler status, of family members who had accompanied the prisoners from need or love or both, and of the children born either on the island or on the lengthy trip to it. Although for many years his claim to have accomplished that task was considered an exaggeration, evidently he did interview ten thousand people, recording for each his or her name, age, religion, birthplace, and so on.

In mid-October, T. left for home with his census cards. He returned around the continent, instead of across it, in a leisurely voyage by sea—which makes one realize that he could also have reached Sakhalin by such a route, thus avoiding much hardship and solitary travel. Both before and after his experiences in the penal colony, he knew moments of extraordinary happiness which found physical expression in love; on the homeward journey this moment came during a stopover on Ceylon, a tropical island as different from the bleak Sakhalin as it is possible to imagine, where he made love "with a black-eyed Hindu girl." Finally back home in December, he wrote an acquaintance that he would feel no injustice were he to die of dysentery or suffer a paralytic stroke, for "*I have lived!* That will do for me!"

That his expedition to and from the colony didn't really "do" for him is clear from the fact that he set off on another lengthy, though more conventional, trip—to cities in Western Europe—soon after his euphoria dissipated. Nevertheless, the adventure seems to have abetted both his physical and spiritual health and to have contributed to the increased depth of his writing: in the fourteen years remaining to him, he accomplished the work upon which his present reputation is most firmly based. The book that is the most obvious consequence of the journey has had little influence upon his reputation, however—even though it is by far his longest work. It is as objective a record as T. could put together of what he saw and experienced on Sakhalin, as well as a distillation of his extensive reading about the island in scientific and penal literature. Liberals of later generations have believed that this book of T.'s affected social attitudes, and helped bring about an amelio-

ration of the harsh treatment of convicts in his country; if
so, its reverberations were minor enough that it remained
untranslated into English for almost seventy-five years.

T. died in his forty-fourth year, succumbing at last to
the tuberculosis that he contracted long before his trip,
roughly at the time of his early popularity as a writer of
humorous tales. His census cards are preserved in the
Lenin Library, named for the revolutionary leader who
some years after T.'s death toppled the autocracy and assumed power. Lenin was ruthless in the pursuit of a pure
and hence unobtainable political idea; had T. lived, he
would have found the new tyranny much more appalling
than the old, for his own pursuit was of a personal and
artistic freedom so complete or absolute that it is a meta-
physical desire.

T. was, of course, an actual person, a writer of stories
and plays who also happened to be a physician; but I honor
the man too much to call him by name throughout an
account that—despite my extensive reliance on his correspondence, his creative work, his book about the island,
and the various biographies in English devoted to him—is
bound (especially in those earlier chapters in which I
would show him caught in human entanglements for which
there are hints but no precise records, such as the ones he
kept of his experiences on the island) to be a fiction of my
own, one in which dialogue must be invention and many
scenes an embellishment of facts. To reconstruct his journey is to acknowledge its influence on me, its continuing
hold on my imagination, feelings, and personal experience;
in such subjective matters, there always exists the possibility of misreading from a personal need. Since I have never
visited any portion of his immense nation, the landscape
across which he will travel in my narrative will have to be
the landscape of my own dreams, as modified by his descriptions. A further reason exists for avoiding his name—
T.'s own wish to escape adulation and public scrutiny. It is

an aspect of that impulse toward the anonymity of pure freedom which I find crucial to an understanding of his trip. To refer to him simply by initial is in keeping with my intuited comprehension of his nature as well as a means of maintaining a distance necessary to me if I am to write of him at all. (Other people in my account, including members of T.'s family, friends, professional acquaintances, and the like, matter less, and so I can call them by their diminutive or Anglicized names, such as Masha or Nicholas.) The initial T. comes from an early transliteration of his name in English. At the time his work became popular in England—it was during the first World War, and his country was an ally of unknown quality: his stories became a medium for reaching the "soul" or "life" of a people so unfamiliar or different as to appear exotic—the first syllable of his last name was spelled "Tche," something like a little cough or sneeze.

His name was spelled this way in the worn copy of a translation of his letters I found more than a decade ago in the British Institute library in Florence. I was familiar with his stories—indeed, I felt so close to some of them that I believed I could tell, despite my inability to read his language, if a phrase or sentence were botched in the translation—, but knew very little about his life, and it was from the letters that I first learned about his trip to the island. The volume I borrowed from the library had a prefatory biographical sketch, based on a memoir of T.'s brother Michael, written in an English so ingenuous it reminded me of one of my children's long since discarded phonograph records, in which José Ferrer narrates the youthful career of the prodigy Mozart. Artlessness has always appealed to me: sentences like "Wolfgang labored night and day," briskly accompanied by the music which is the fruit of that labor; or, in the tattered pages of the Illustrated Classics version of *Richard II* that my oldest son once owned, the words of the assassin as he stabs Richard, "Take that, Dick Plantagenet!"

In Florence, recovering during a sabbatical leave from the exhaustion occasioned by a year of racial turmoil at my university in upstate New York, I was particularly attracted by whatever was artlessly limpid, like the preface to the letters of T. From that biographical sketch, I learned that T.'s father was born a serf, and that his grandfather "purchased his freedom and the freedom of his family" from the nobleman to whom they belonged, "with one daughter, Alexandra, thrown in for nothing." T.'s father eventually became a merchant in a provincial town, prospered for a time, and married the daughter of another merchant. The couple had five boys and one girl, T. being the third son. The father "was always inclined to neglect his business. He took an active interest in all the affairs of the town, devoted himself to church singing, conducted the choir, played the violin, and painted ikons." He trained his children to be a choir in their own right, taught them to play the violin, and hired for them a piano teacher and also a French governess to provide lessons in foreign languages—much as if they belonged to the nobility. "The father was severe, and even went so far as to chastise"— i.e., whip—"his children, but they all lived on warm and affectionate terms. . . . Every Saturday the whole family went to the evening service, and on their return sang hymns and burned incense. On Sunday morning they went to early mass, after which they all sang hymns at home." The pious authoritarianism and status-seeking of the father was offset by the gentleness of the mother, who "instilled into her children a hatred of brutality and a feeling of regard for all who were in an inferior position and for birds and animals."

One doesn't find language like that in the later biographies, which reflect the greater psychological sophistication of our age. And yet it was the very innocence of that language which enabled me to find certain affinities between T.'s parents and my own. My mother was similar to T.'s, as the latter is captured in those few phrases; my father was neither pious nor much of a disciplinarian, but, like T.'s, was rendered impractical by a passion to rise in the world. Both men failed in business; both lost houses beyond their means and fled from creditors, leaving their families behind.

T.'s older brothers reestablished the family in Moscow, but T. remained, to finish his high school education; continuing to live in the house, which now belonged to one of the creditors, he supported himself by tutoring. One of his pupils, who became a friend, was the creditor's nephew.

Following his reunion with his family in Moscow, T.'s story rapidly becomes one of success, of that upward mobility we think of—perhaps less so now than in previous epochs—as uniquely American. In partial explanation of that climb, the sketch speaks of the emergence, soon after T.'s birth, of "the educated middle class," the one which he (whatever his dislike of social categories) was privileged to enter, to some degree through the past endeavors of his father and grandfather; and of the general capacity of people in his country "for completely changing their way of life." Later in my year in Florence I read in a more scholarly text of the reforms of the 1860s, which, in addition to liberating the serfs (often to a peasant hardship greater than they had suffered in bondage), modernized the judicial system, gave greater administrative autonomy to the districts, provided (at least in theory) free health services, and enabled young people not of the aristocracy to go on to the university and therefore enter, often with considerable idealism, the expanding fields of education, law, medicine, and the various arts.

Despite their poverty, T. and his brothers all went to the university; his sister, unable to attend because of her sex, enrolled in an advanced course of study for women. In reading of their efforts, I was reminded (the analogy is far from precise) of my own Depression generation. Young people of that generation, believing in Franklin D.

Roosevelt and in liberal reform, were encouraged by parents who had at best a high school education to go on to college, to achieve new dreams. Indeed, in that Depression era, many children simply assumed their right to a higher education, though nobody knew how the cost was to be borne: paradoxically, anything seemed possible in those bleak days. Such optimism—a belief in a future that would redeem the present—may not have prevailed among all the members of T.'s family, but it clearly did with T., and he carried that. optimism to his grave. Each child had to help support the family (one rebelled, and moved elsewhere) and yet find the money for his or her education. T., who accepted the major responsibility for the family's welfare almost immediately upon his arrival in Moscow, discovered he could most readily earn an income while studying medicine by writing brief stories for the popular journals. In fact, he continued to write after he completed his studies, finding literature more profitable than his medical practice. T.'s sister and one of his brothers became teachers; of the other brothers, one (who had studied law) became a tax official, one a journalist, one an artist.

By the time T. made his decision, at age thirty, to visit the penal colony, he was already well known, a recipient of the most prestigious literary award of his country—one of the first major Russian writers to come from a class other than the nobility. And for the first time in his life he felt as if he were escaping servitude. In a letter to his friend and publisher Alexis Suvorin the year preceding his trip—it is not referred to in the sketch, but is included in the volume—, he says that a writer needs more than "plenty of material and talent": he needs maturity and "the feeling of personal freedom" (his underlining), a feeling that "has only recently begun to develop in me. . . . What writers belonging to the upper class have received from nature for nothing, plebians acquire at the cost of their youth." And then he summarizes a story—clearly his own—as a narrative his friend might develop:

Write a story of how a young man, the son of a serf, who has served in a shop, sung in a choir, been at a high school and a university, who has been brought up to respect everyone of higher rank and position, to kiss priests' hands, to reverence other people's ideas, to be thankful for every morsel of bread, who has been many times whipped, who has trudged from one pupil to another without galoshes, who has been used to fighting, and tormenting animals, who has liked dining with his rich relations, and been hypocritical before God and men from the mere consciousness of his own insignificance—write how this young man squeezes the slave out of himself, drop by drop, and how waking one beautiful morning he feels that he has no longer a slave's blood in his veins but a real man's.

What, then, accounts for the severity of T.'s depression, and for the concomitant need to make a difficult and sometimes dangerous journey through a largely unpopulated continent to an island not magical, like Prospero's; not one which would grant him governance and the trappings of power, like Sancho's; not to any island invested with the glorious flora and fauna of the imagination, but rather to a real and barely habitable island of ignorance, brutality, and slavery, on which those with the fiercest impulse toward freedom were chained to an iron ball or a wheelbarrow?

2

It is March 9, 1890. Let us make it late evening, a good time for reading a periodical or a book, or for writing letters. T. and the members of the family living with him have eaten the dinner the cook has prepared, and the maid has cleared the table. The house, which they have occupied for nearly four years, is on Sadovaya-Kudrinskaya Street, in a fashionable district. T. sits before his desk in the first-floor doctor's office that also is his study, writing a letter to his friend Suvorin, who lives in Petersburg. The other first-floor rooms consist of the kitchen, the servants' quarters, and bedrooms for T. and his youngest brother, Michael. On the second floor are the living and dining rooms, and the bedrooms of T.'s mother and sister. (The father, Paul, lives elsewhere, to be closer, he says, to his job: he has relinquished family authority to T., who pays the bills, and as a consequence feels awkward at home. And yet he is proud of T.—almost as proud of him as he is of his son

Ivan, who, as chief official of a public school, wears a uniform with brass buttons and a hat with a cockade. What he finds most distressing about his third son is T.'s open rejection of religion.) The love of music is one legacy of his father that T. will never renounce; the living room contains a rented piano. On the wall hangs a large painting by T.'s brother Nicholas of a seamstress who has fallen asleep at dawn over her work; like that work, the canvas itself is unfinished, Nicholas having died nine months previously of the illness that also afflicts T.

The mother is, say, in the living room, sewing, while Michael—Misha, to the family—is half-drowsing on the settee. Mary—Masha—is playing the piano for her own amusement and for them, but is conscious of the fact that the sound of it will faintly reach T., even though his door downstairs is closed; she knows that T. likes the sound of distant music as he writes. These three are T.'s most ardent supporters. His mother, who can barely write herself, finds a "gleam of glory" on the face of this son who has gained fame for whatever it is he is always putting on paper. She is extremely emotional, and this radiance—as well as much else that she alone perceives—causes her eyes to fill with tears. Mary already displays the readiness to devote herself to T.'s well-being and to the advancement of his career that will ultimately result in her rejection of several suitors and in the jealousy and hurt she will feel when T., three years before his death, marries an actress—and does so without consulting, or even informing, her. As for Michael, T. has always been his model, partly because T. is closer to his age than are the two oldest brothers, Alexander and the now-dead Nicholas; and partly because T. has always seemed to him more reliable and affectionate than they. In emulation of T., Michael has begun to write some stories of his own; his enduring contributions as a writer, though, will be two books whose central concern is his favorite brother.

At his desk, T. is trying to answer Suvorin's latest

objections to his forthcoming trip. He begins firmly: "We are both mistaken about Sakhalin, but you are probably more mistaken than I am. I am going there absolutely secure in the thought that my journey will not make any valuable contributions to literature and science: I have neither the knowledge, time, nor pretensions for that." It is easier, of course, to make negative assertions than positive ones; he pauses, runs a hand through his hair, and sighs. All the pictures I have seen of T. in his early manhood show him as slender and athletic, and suggest a concern for appearance. Certainly he wears clothes with grace, and they seem tailored to his tall frame. Nothing about him hints of illness. The verbal descriptions are similar, and emphasize in addition the expressiveness of his eyes, a characteristic perhaps inherited from his mother. (T. has said of himself and his brothers and sister—he is so quoted in that sketch based on Michael's memoir—, "Our talents we got from our father, but our heart from our mother." The extremely gifted oldest brother, Alexander, a journalist in Petersburg who despises his work, who has never forgiven Paul for his warden-like discipline and for the disgrace he has brought to the family, and who blames his own dissoluteness and lack of achievement upon the father, considers T.'s remark much too generous.) I see T. as erect in his chair, still wearing the coat, almost as long as a cloak, that he put on for dinner; except for his trimmed beard and more mature bone structure, he looks much as he did in the portrait Nicholas made of him as a university student: eyes dark and contemplative, a tangled lock of hair fallen over the left one.

He starts to write again, rapidly and without thought to his contradictions. He hopes the trip will result in a book that will "pay off some of my debt to medicine, toward which, as you know, I've behaved like a pig." (He has frequently confessed to this friend his guilt for not writing the medical thesis his university degree requires, and for scribbling stories at the expense of his practice.) "I may not be able to write anything at all, but the journey still retains its charm for me. . . . Granted, my journey may be trifling, hardheaded, capricious, but think a while and tell me what I stand to lose by going. Time? Money? Will I suffer hardships?" His time is "worth nothing and I never have money anyway"; as for hardships, they are inconsequential, and, besides, he needs "six months' continuous physical and mental labor" for the sake of self-discipline. "Granted, I may get nothing out of it, but there are sure to be two or three days out of the whole trip that I'll remember all my life with rapture or bitterness."

Rapture or bitterness: one or the other of these opposites, but not the struggle between them that mutes each. The conflict is between those rare moments of extreme happiness which comes with the transcendence of self—this is, after all, the freedom T. aspires to—and those perhaps more common moments in which the self, having swollen to become the world, has nothing external upon which to spread its corrosive resentment, the objects or people it seemingly holds in contempt being but its extensions. His brother Alexander lives constantly in such a state, while T. himself has lately been fending it off with a cheer that is hypocritical. How does one avoid nullity, a paralysis of the soul? In invoking his antithetical pair, T. has touched upon his deepest anxiety, and his language at once takes on an almost angry urgency. His explanations so far, he says to Suvorin, "may be unconvincing, but what you write is just as unconvincing," and then comes that grand rhetoric which has served to explain his trip to generations of liberals:

> You write, for instance, that Sakhalin is of no use or interest to anyone. Is that really so? Sakhalin could be of no use or interest only to a society that doesn't deport thousands of people to it and doesn't spend millions on it. Except for Australia in the past and Cayenne, Sakhalin is the only place where the use of

convicts for colonization can be studied. All Europe is
interested in it, and we don't find it of any use? Not
more than twenty-five to thirty years ago our own
Russians performed astounding feats in the explora-
tion of Sakhalin, feats that are enough to make you
want to deify man, but we have no use for it, we don't
even know who those people were, and all we do is sit
within our four walls and complain what a mess God
has made of creating man. Sakhalin is a place of unbearable suffering, the sort of suffering only man,
whether free or subjugated, is capable of. The people
who work near it or on it have been trying to solve
problems involving frightening responsibility; they
are still trying. I'm sorry I'm not sentimental or I'd
say that we ought to make pilgrimages to places like
Sakhalin the way the Turks go to Mecca. . . . From the
books I've read and am now reading, it is evident that
we have let *millions* of people rot in jails, we have let
them rot to no purpose, unthinkingly and barbar-
ously. We have driven people through the cold, in
chains, across tens of thousands of versts, we have
infected them with syphilis, debauched them, bred
criminals and blamed it all on red-nosed prison wardens. Now all educated Europe knows that all of us,
not the wardens, are to blame, but it's still none of our
business; it's of no interest to us. The much-glorified
sixties did *nothing* for the sick and the people in prison
and thereby violated the chief commandment of
Christian civilization. In our time a few things are
being done for the sick, but nothing at all for the
prisoners; prison management holds absolutely no interest for our jurists. No, I assure you, Sakhalin is of
great use and interest, and the only sad part of it all is
that I'm the one who's going and not someone more
conversant with the problems and capable of arousing
public interest. I myself am going there on a trivial
pretext.

It is difficult to attack either one's country or one's father and be without bitterness: even the idealism which may be the basis of the censure nourishes the resentful and swelling self. In his moral lecture on the significance of Sakhalin, T. is attacking both a fatherland and a surrogate parent. He is deeply attached to the person to whom his strictures are addressed; in many respects, Suvorin is the kind of older friend who serves as the ideal father. That is to say, he has advised and encouraged T. and has used his considerable influence as a person and publisher to raise T. in the public esteem; he may even have had a backstage role in the presentation to T. of his highest award, the Pushkin Prize. Like T.'s family, Suvorin has come from humble stock; both he and T. are grandsons of serfs. Suvorin has succeeded in every way that T.'s own father has failed. A liberal in his youth, Suvorin nevertheless has become increasingly conservative as his wealth and prestige have grown. T. never has permitted the political attitudes of another to interfere with friendship; he refuses to consider himself either a liberal or a conservative, since any such label would restrict his sense of himself. And yet it now seems obvious to him that Suvorin would defend a comfortable status quo regardless of the harm it brought to others. In his opposition to T.'s proposed journey, he is blind to social injustice and the suffering of unfortunates; he has become as narrow as Paul. . ...

Perhaps my love of T. is narcissistic; perhaps he is but a mirror of my ideal self. I am drawn to him, I know, in his passionate remarks about Sakhalin, by his obvious attempt to avoid righteousness and the puffing up of his own ego. He senses the danger; his wings are flapping to help him rise above himself into the pure air of freedom which a year ago in a moment of newfound confidence he felt himself finally attaining. It may be that his own rhetoric has convinced him that he has gained that air, and has no further need to struggle to stay aloft; it is just as likely that he considers his rhetoric corrupt, sullied by the hostility that

underlies it, and is unsure of his grasp on any moral truth.
Whatever the reason, as he turns to another topic—student
disturbances—he plummets, as if the air is too thin to support him. Assuming a political position that he knows to
be congenial to his friend, he writes:

> We've been having some grandiose student disorders.
> It all began with the Academy of Peter the Great when
> the administration prohibited students from taking
> girls to official dormitory rooms, suspecting the girls
> not only of prostitution, but of politics as well. From
> the Academy it spread to the University, where stu-
> dents, surrounded by heavily armed Hectors and
> Achilleses, mounted and bearing lances, are now de-
> manding the following:
>
> 1. Complete autonomy for universities.
> 2. Complete academic freedom.
> 3. Free admission to the university without re-
>   gard to religion, nationality, sex or social
>   status.
> 4. Admission of Jews to the university without
>   any restrictions, in addition to granting them
>   rights equal to those of other students.
> 5. Freedom of assembly and recognition of stu-
>   dent associations.
> 6. Establishment of a university and student tri-
>   bunal.
> 7. Abolition of school inspectors' police func-
>   tions.
> 8. Lowering of tuition.
>
> I copied this with a few abridgments from a
> leaflet. I think the flames are being fanned most vehe-
> mently by a bunch of young Jews and by the sex that
> is dying to get into the university, though five times
> worse prepared than the men, while even the men are

miserably prepared and with rare exceptions make abominable students.

Coming so soon after an exalted declaration of humanitarianism, this passage is astonishing. However ill-prepared the students may be, he is attacking them for desiring the freedom and social justice he himself desires; in such an attack, he is eroding his own freedom and undermining that which he honors most in himself. He is neither an anti-Semite nor what in our era is called a male chauvinist; his life before the writing of this letter and afterwards shows him fighting discrimination and spite wherever he finds them. His friendship with Suvorin, for example, is to be strained by the Dreyfus Affair: T. will be appalled that Suvorin's newspaper supports the anti-Semitic position of those conservatives and reactionaries throughout Europe who applaud the secret court-martial, however trumped-up they know the charges to be, that has sent Dreyfus to Devil's Island—to the Cayenne of T.'s present letter, the penal colony he sees as comparable to Sakhalin.

The volume of T.'s letters I found in Florence faithfully records the gossipy irony—how I dislike seeing similar phrases in my own handwriting in a letter left open on a table by some friend I am visiting!—that precedes the listing of the student demands, but omits those much more damaging sentences that follow it; and this whole section about the students is ignored by those who would discover in T.'s journey to the island nothing but an overwhelming need to be of service to mankind. At nearly the midpoint of the 1960s, that decade of even more large-scale student disorders than those T. refers to, an activist-minded American literary critic chastised a black novelist for not being the kind of artist that T. was: T., "probably as devoted to the purity of art" as that novelist, "dragged himself from a sick-bed to visit the penal colony of Sakhalin

Island and speak to the conscience of his country about the tormented prisoners. Other writers have done similar deeds, for they have felt obliged to live not merely as writers but also as men engaged with the problems and passions of their time. . . . All I would like to say is that his trip to Sakhalin was, for him, necessary and, in my view of things, noble."

At his desk, writing his letter of contradictory explanations to Suvorin, T. looks quite unlike a man who has just dragged himself from a sick-bed. He does feel that his trip is a necessary one, but his first and overriding motive is a personal need for exile and escape. His thought is, Why do I feel my own worthlessness so? The death of Nicholas, the first in his family to die, no longer grieves him, but is a threat to his own meaning and becomes part of everything that disturbs him—his obsequiousness as a child, his pleasure even now at somebody's praise or flattery, the severity of his past moral pronouncements to the two older brothers, the living and the dead, for their disorderly lives. His own reputation is meaningless, for he knows how far his achievements are from what he wants to accomplish; fame inspires in him no confidence in the society that bestows it. Fame is a ribbon, a medal, a check. Fame engenders envy on the part of those, perhaps just as meritorious, who have not been singled out, and poisonous attacks from critics who favor writers with political positions closer to their own. Fame results in countless requests of favors from people whose deepest desire is a medal for themselves.

Physician though he is, T. refuses to admit that coughing up blood—and once more he has suffered such a spasm, just a few nights ago—is a sign of consumption, his brother's mortal disease; he suffers, rather, from thinking too much. He desires to defeat his anomie. He wants to be kind, to be gentle; he will close his letter with words of comfort and affection for Suvorin, who has been worrying about his advancing years and the prospect of senility.

"Keep well and content," he writes. "I am as willing to believe in your old age as in the fourth dimension." As he continues with his words of encouragement ("You think and work enough for ten people. . . , old age is bad only for bad old people and difficult only for the difficult, and you're a good person who is not difficult"), he hears, for the first time, the piano: Mary, a sensitive and intelligent member of that sex denied admission to the university, is deftly playing—the School of Advanced Studies for Women encourages its girls to be proficient in the arts—a work by an eminent composer who lately has been writing letters of admiration to T. for his stories.

For a moment, T. cannot make his pen move. It is as if he is caught between his love for Mary, for Michael, for his mother, for others in his family and those who, like Suvorin, seem to belong to it—a love which, as it reaches beyond the men and women he is most intimate with, out to a desolate and fog-enshrouded island thousands of miles away, becomes more rarefied and abstract, transforming itself into the compassion we sometimes have for the ephemeral smidgens that constitute the goddamned human race, the brutal and the brutalized alike, each in the intensity of desire believing him or herself at the very center of a universe terrifying in its immensity and indifference to all of us—; caught between such a love, with its accompanying pity, and a bitterness, a self-contempt, which makes any suggestion of love returned to him, any hint of admiration for his "goodness" or talent, something so suffocating that his actual breathing becomes labored and painful. Here is how he ends his letter: "The difference between youth and age is quite relative and dependent on convention. And with this, out of respect for you, allow me to fling myself into a deep gorge and smash my skull to smithereens."

3

———

Rarely can we so accurately determine the moment of decision for a major action in a life as we can that for T.'s journey to the penal colony. One day in the fall of 1889, he picked up some notes that were part of Michael's preparation for a civil-service examination on criminal law and prison management. In his memoir, Michael says that T., after glancing at the notes, told him: "All our attention is centered on the criminal up to the moment when sentence is pronounced, but as soon as he is sent to prison, we forget about him entirely. But what happens in prison? I can imagine!" The notes contained a reference to Sakhalin—Michael had jotted down something about it he'd heard in a class lecture—and T. told his brother he intended to go there; the decision was so sudden that Michael thought he was joking. As a schoolboy, T. had been fascinated by Ivan Goncharov's *Frigate Pallas*, a book describing a voyage that included the far eastern islands, but this and a story by Vladimir Korolenko about the escape of some prisoners from Sakhalin was the apparent extent of his knowledge of, or interest in, that remote region.

All expeditions, including those to the moon—expeditions in which one or a group of individuals renounces civilization for the sake of the unknown—, become, in the imagination of those left behind, metaphors of their own individual desires or proclivities. The metaphorical quality is enhanced by sojourners who, like T., remain elusive in their explanations of what they're after. If T.'s trek across a continent is a parable of the engaged artist, of one who will battle for the betterment of humanity at whatever cost to his health and art, it is also, for the romantically inclined, the flight of a good man from a hopeless passion for a married woman. Writing, long after T. was safely dead, of his first meeting with her, the originator of this legend says, "We just looked closely into each other's eyes, but what a lot it meant! It seemed as if my soul had exploded and a rocket had soared aloft; brightly, joyously, triumphantly, ecstatically." She declares she had "not the remotest doubt" that T. "felt the same as we looked at each other in amazement and delight." Although one can more readily imagine a writer like T. fleeing over a vast tundra to escape someone capable of such prose than to carry his passion for her into exile, her example has led others to search for a hidden sexual reason for the trip—if not a relationship with a woman, then one with a man: might not T.'s affection for Suvorin have contained a homosexual element troubling to him? Did he not always manage to elude—at least until he was near the end of his life—the many attractive women who were mad for more than a passing affair with him? Good scholars, who dismiss all such reasons with the contempt they give to Marxist interpretations of him as an advance comrade of the revolution, have no difficulty in assuming that T.'s chief motive, whatever his undeniable humanitarianism, was that unfinished dissertation: any impeccable researcher

knows the lengths to which another like him will go in
order to obtain the necessary data. And—to bring this ar-
bitrary list to a close—a writer who was on friendly terms
with T., particularly in the latter's final years, finds in the
trip the suicidal tendency that surfaced again a decade later
in the marriage his health simply couldn't afford.

If I would pause over that last theory, although I don't
wholly accept it, I do so partly because it bears upon an
experience of my own, and partly because of the supporting evidence in the letters T. wrote in the months preceding
his departure—particularly the extraordinarily bitter one
to an editor whose journal had just listed him among "the
high priests of unprincipled writing." In this letter, T.'s
reference to his trip is as brief as it is significant. Usually,
he says, he does not respond to criticism, "but in this
instance, it seems to be a question not of criticism, but of
libel, pure and simple. I might have let even libel go by,
except that in a few days I will be leaving Russia for an
extended period, perhaps never to return. . . ." Was he
considering the possibility that the trip might bring his
death? Or had editors and critics so angered him that he
envisioned a life of permanent exile? Perhaps all that one
can say with certainty is that at this moment T. wants to
escape—he wants out, at whatever the personal cost. The
desire for absolute freedom—and for the honor, truth, dignity, human justice, and all the rest of the virtues that
would accompany its impossible achievement—can carry
us to that immovable and eternal region, small as the small-
est bleached bone of a finger or with the unspeakable immensity of the universe, in which desire itself is silent.

Whatever its documentation, the metaphor developed
in the following pages is my own, and is, I suppose, as self-
serving as anybody else's—even though it first came to me
with the certainty granted by old but buried knowledge
and with all the elegance of a mathematical equation that
solves an abstruse problem. It came to me in Florence, at a
time I most needed it, as a consequence of my reading of

T.'s stories and the letters he wrote during the journey. After I returned to the United States, I discovered that a translation of T.'s book about Sakhalin had been published, and in reading it I felt the elation that one has in finding validation for whatever one already accepts as truth. The dead are at the mercy of the living, but the mercy which proceeds from the dead can grace those yet alive, and provide a purer air for their breathing.

4

At 8:00 P.M. on April 21, under a sky black with imminent rain, the train for Yaroslavl, a city on the Volga River, left the drafty station at Moscow on schedule, as is often the case under despotic rule. Among the passengers were T. and a group of his friends and relatives who had come along for this first leg of a journey he was making to what seemed to them the edge of the world. The relatives were his small and frightened mother, Eugenia; his sister, Mary, and two of his brothers, Michael and Ivan. These family members sat with T. in one of the compartments, along with as many of the friends as could squeeze in; others sat in the neighboring compartment or on one or another of the pieces of T's luggage in the corridor. Of his friends, Isaac was a landscape painter already become something of

26

a celebrity; Sophia, an amateur painter; Dr. Kuvshinnikov, a medical examiner for the Moscow Police Department; two younger men, Marian and Alexander, musicians; Olga, a mathematician; and Lika, a young schoolteacher.

Sophia sat opposite T., between her husband, who was the police doctor, and Isaac, who was her lover. It is not surprising that the first name of the compliant Dr. Kuvshinnikov, a man content to melt into the crowd of artists his wife required for her happiness, has been ignored by T's biographers. Isaac was Jewish and a notorious womanizer who preferred cheerful, even slightly foolish, women like Sophia, for with them he could be however he pleased—autocratic and demanding, charming, melancholy, or sullen—and could pass each of them on to someone else without a scruple.

The other four took turns sitting on the luggage in the corridor or retreating to the neighboring compartment, where they had to sit with strangers. The musicians, close friends, were somewhat like Sophia in their need for conviviality; but, unlike her, they required no home. Rootless, they drifted from party to party, and were serious about nothing but their music. Marian, a cellist and orchestra member, was a native of Poland. Alexander, a flutist, taught at the Moscow Conservatory. Whenever these two drank too much, they argued about the relative merits of composers and the correct interpretations of their works. Even if such a debate began with an important point, it quickly became so absurd that the winner was the one capable of the most preposterous claim. Usually, Alexander won; he took pride in his imagination, and between performances and Conservatory teaching would dash off poetic stories of little merit.

Olga, the most intellectual of the lot, had a boisterous laugh, little care for her appearance, and a radical bent in politics that might have been the reason she had lost her job as a statistician in the state astronomical observatory. Lika was a girl of such exceptional beauty that it gave men, including Isaac, a shyness in her presence, for the desire she aroused in them made them feel inferior to the goodness or perfection they found in her; and she herself was shy, as if, for example, her long ash-blond hair was a gift that should have been bestowed on another—she was always brushing wisps of it from her eyes in a self-conscious manner.

Lika adored T.; but, being unable to reveal her passion to him during her many visits to the house on Sadovaya-Kudrinskaya Street, she concentrated her attention on his sister, to whom she gave embraces and smiles mysterious to Mary. Now she sat close to Olga in the compartment occupied also by a priest and a businessman. Knowing of the older woman's belief in, and loyalty to, T., Lika was almost as fond of her as she was of Mary. Olga's emotions, as well as her intellectual convictions, were announced to the world at large, and Lika admired her frankness the way we admire all that is vital and that we can never be: tropical birds, lions, ballet dancers, actresses. But whenever Olga behaved too outrageously—for example, she had just said *Do you think Antosha* (an affectionate diminutive for T. that should have been used only by his mother) *will be shocked to find that I'm going with him on the boat?* and then had laughed with such a series of snorts that the other occupants stared at her—Lika blushed; and that specific remark made her wish she had the courage either to board the river steamer too, or to get off the train at the next stop.

What an assemblage of people, talented and otherwise, conventional and unconventional, pious and scornful of religion! Perhaps the friends were so diverse because T. had not sought them out; they had become his acquaintances after first becoming intimate with another member of his family. Despite the differences in their ages—Sophia was almost forty, Olga thirty, Lika barely twenty—, all the women had been Mary's fellow students at the Academy of Advanced Studies; most of the men had been fellow students or drinking companions of T.'s artist brother Nicholas, whose alcoholism had hastened his death from consumption the previous year. A person whose friends come to him through a sister and a brother is apt on some level to be elusive, as if his needs extend beyond human intercourse; and his gaiety and gregariousness can seem but a wish to pass the time in a manner agreeable to others. On this two-hundred-fifty-mile trip they were making for his sake, T.'s friends—even after he had rummaged through his biggest bag for his new boots smelling of tar and his heavy leather coat and had put them on to stalk up and down the corridor and into the next compartment with his sheathed knife clenched between his teeth as if he were a pirate—felt not only as though they were excluded from his thoughts, but as though they really did not know him.

It had been Sophia's idea to have a portable seeing-off party; and, as with the parties that many in this group regularly attended at the Kuvshinnikov house, her husband had been responsible for the food and refreshments, which remained unopened in the picnic basket awkwardly straddled by his feet. This particular party was not going very well because T. was attending to the anxieties and fears of his own family and ignoring the concerns of his friends. To them, particularly to Sophia, his mad journey seemed both a rejection of friendship and an unaccountable personal threat, as if they were trivial or foolish persons, their lives commonplace.

Sophia overheard T. instructing the stolid Ivan—imagine, he was wearing his headmaster's coat as if this were a school outing!—about some detail of their mother's planned visit to a monastery after they said goodbye to T. at Yaroslavl: she was going there to rest and to pray for his safety. "Now, don't pray too much, Mother," Sophia heard T. saying as he turned from Ivan to grasp her hand. "It's bad for your leg to bend it." He was of course teasing her, but his mother looked alarmed as if not praying were

inconceivable to her: what then might happen to her Antosha? And, to demonstrate the soundness of her limbs,
she quickly raised both legs three times, looking at him
triumphantly.

"If your leg is so good, why did you bring *that?*" T.
asked gently, pointing to the cane at her side. "To shame
you for leaving her, Anton Pavlovich," Sophia answered,
for somebody had to break up this little family consulta-
tion: if only the mother and Ivan had stayed home! "To
pull you back at the last minute," Isaac said, reaching
across the aisle for the cane. "None of us wants you to go,
you see," and, putting the crook around T.'s neck, he gave
the cane a slightly malicious tug.

"No, no," the practical-minded Dr. Kuvshinnikov
protested, in reference simply to the purpose of the cane;
he had sensed the grievance in his wife's words and the
restlessness in Isaac's response, and had perceived T.'s resentment—his face had reddened—at being held by the
neck, like a prisoner, and he wished to soothe them all.
"It's a real contusion, she bruised her leg God knows
how—a fall against a sharp object, the edge of a stool perhaps. . . . The cane is a necessity." Having given his professional opinion, he was ashamed of his temerity, and added,
almost shyly, stroking his mustache, "As to the frequency
of her prayers—" here he looked at T.'s mother with a
coyness that was almost flirtatious "—that question must
be answered by a higher physician than Anton or I."

"Oh, darling, how sweet you are!" cried Sophia in
delight; it did seem to her that a true party might be beginning, for her husband often served as a catalyst to a conversation that left him far behind. And Dr. Kuvshinnikov,
smiling benignly, patted both his wife and Isaac on the
knee, and bent forward across the aisle to do the same with
T. and Eugenia. This business with the cane seemed to him
an unpleasant pother over nothing but the fact that T. was
leaving them; and yet, to be truthful, he himself felt a
certain reproachfulness toward T. How he had enjoyed—

at one or another of those parties at which people were upsetting vases with their clumsy somersaults or talking with intoxication of the latest painter in France—his own conversations with T. about, say, the autopsy he had performed that morning!

Instead of acknowledging Dr. Kuvshinnikov's conciliatory gesture or paying the slightest attention to Sophia or Isaac, T. was speaking privately to his sister, who seemed as ready to break into tears as his mother. In Dr. Kuvshinnikov's opinion, T. was suffering a nervous disorder of the kind that afflicts people of undue sensitivity—artists, chiefly—as they reach their thirtieth year. It was soon after her thirtieth birthday that Sophia became pale and bored and started to lose weight, not because of anything physical—her heart and lungs were sound—but because her art required her to be a free spirit. Her parties, her affairs, immediately brought back her appetite. Well, so be it, then! A doctor must not permit self-interest to interfere with a cure. And yet, back home after a weekend with Isaac or some other man, she would be miserable, begging his forgiveness, decrying her talent, lacerating her soul for the misery and anxiety she had caused him. Aware of her expenditures for a fashionable coat or dress, she would impulsively fire the cook and become as sensible of the cost of poultry or fish as any clerk's wife. "I will be faithful to my poor darling," she would say sadly, while the house filled with smoke from the hen she was burning in her attempt to be domestic. It was unbearable to him that she, an artist, had to breathe that oppressive smoke while her eyes so brimmed with tears she couldn't tell the salt from the sugar; and yet her periods of suffering were apparently necessary to give meaning to her weekends away and perhaps—though it was too deep for him—to impart universality to her artistic vision, which Isaac called tragic. "You must fulfill yourself," he implored her whenever she sighed and put on an apron. "Come, be a free spirit again!"

Dr. Kuvshinnikov had always thought of T. as a professional colleague—a man much too level-headed to be an artist, whatever the surprising attention that came to him for his stories and plays. But in the past month T. had rudely ignored his friends, being buried (he said) in books about Sakhalin; and then, in apparent contrition for his solitude, had invited everybody to a suddenly-called dinner party. On such occasions, T.'s words were apt to be at odds with the topic of conversation. "Yes, Australia is very far away," he once said in response to Dr. Kuvshinnikov's remark about the fragility of the clavicle. Only very recently, though, had Dr. Kuvshinnikov been made aware of the possible enormity of T's behavior, of an irresponsibility so great that it implied genius of the most tormented kind. To no normal human could the police doctor speak as he now did to T. He leaned forward and asked almost reverently, "Is it true, Anton, what I have heard?"

"What's that?"

"I pity you your anguish."

"For what?"

"Your mother is going to the monastery. Just for a rest, I know. But after that? I say. . . ." He paused, looking significantly at the old woman, who was dozing. "And the others in your little household? One should never trust to what a discharged servant might say, of course."

"I've discharged no servant, and have no intention of doing so."

"No? I'm glad to hear that. Your cook told our maid her worries."

"What worries did your maid tell you that our cook has?"

"Oh, my friend." Dr. Kuvshinnikov blushed, for everybody except T.—Sophia, Isaac, Mary, Michael, Ivan —was looking at him with curiosity. T. was simply smiling with the politeness one has while withdrawing into a shell: T. despised, he knew, any prying into his private life. It was too late for Dr. Kuvshinnikov to extricate himself. He took a breath and held up two fingers. "One, that you're leaving Moscow, perhaps forever, because you're tired of the infernal gossip—"

"Yes, and now perhaps you have the good sense to see why this would be so."

Never had his colleague treated him with such discourtesy; Dr. Kuvshinnikov almost moaned in his embarrassment. "And t-t-two—" for he was stammering in his haste to get it over with, a haste that made him speak more bluntly than he intended to "—that to pay for your trip you have to give up your house and sell the furniture." Even as he spoke, he knew the wrongness of his words. In speaking together of what their maid had told them, Sophia and he had made inferences that were unfounded; his friend was far too generous to dispossess his family, or for that matter to fire an honest servant, however incompetent. And at the same time that he recognized the wrongness of what he had said, he assumed that he himself had made it come true. That is to say, the awfulness of his own words convinced him that he himself was solely at fault, guilty of such malicious gossip that his good and kind friend T. was throwing his family into the street and heading for certain death in the snow-covered wastes. "Forgive me!" he cried, burying his head in his arms.

Innocently enough, Dr. Kuvshinnikov had probed a bruise far more sensitive than the one on Eugenia's leg, for it was true enough that because of the cost of T.'s expedition and the loss of income it entailed, the family had to leave the crowded but comfortable house they had lived in for so many years, the house that Mary had found for them (wanting it, she thought it probably beyond their means), and which was important not only to her but to the others, including T. himself. Did not he and Mary and Michael and Ivan always carry in their memories the awareness of how, when all of them were children, their father's bankruptcy and disgrace had forced the auctioning of their house and its furnishings?

Of course, Dr. Kuvshinnikov caused an uproar by saying something the family felt, if only to a degree, to be true. Michael amd Mary sprang at once to their brother's defense. Though they would not be entering their professions until the fall, their brother was not leaving them homeless and starving in the meantime, but had scraped together enough money to get the family a cottage in the country for the summer and even—he had gone into debt for that—to provide them with some little jaunts of their own. Ivan, who earned a good salary and had an apartment of his own, simply reddened, puffing out his chest froglike in his tight-fitting headmaster's coat.

Still bowed by his regret, Dr. Kuvshinnikov peered through the wool fuzz of the arm of his coat to see how T. was taking all this, and found it difficult to tell what distressed his friend the most—the knowledge that everybody knew about the forthcoming loss of the house, the prolonged discussion of the family's financial status, or the praise that Michael and Mary accorded him. T. sat as though he were a stranger in the compartment, one who would have preferred to be somewhere else. Despite his humiliation, Dr. Kuvshinnikov was physician enough to observe that T. had begun to shift back and forth on his seat, and, as the protestations ebbed, he asked him sympathetically, "Your hemorrhoids acting up?"

The next day, Sophia told her husband that his bravery in mentioning the house had cleared the air, but Dr. Kuvshinnikov assumed that the accuracy of his diagnosis had more to do with the return of good-natured banter and camaraderie. Who could find ruthless villainy or reckless heroism—in either case, behavior profound enough to threaten another's ideal conception of himself—in one who set off on his adventures not with banners and orations but with an insufferably itching rectum?

In the corridor, Alexander and Marian began to parody each other's instrument, one with off-key soprano pipings and the other with groans that seemed to resonate in his belly; they provided the accompaniment with their make-believe flute and cello as the others sang sentimental songs. Then Isaac and Marian and Sopia recounted stories known to them all, anecdotes about T. that revealed the warmth of their feelings for him. For example, Marian asked Mary if she remembered a trip on another train when they had been traveling to Moscow with T. and Eugenia. It had just so happened that a famous scholar who had been Mary's teacher was in the same car, and Mary had been dreadfully self-conscious, worried that Marian and T., who were in high spirits, would do or say something unseemly in front of this awesome individual. As the scholar passed their compartment, Marian and T. bowed like peasants before Mary, crying out that they hoped her charge—the unfortunate Eugenia—would indeed find a job as a maid or cook when she arrived in the great city. The joke so hurt Mary that T. spent the rest of the journey trying to apologize. "How silly I was," Mary now said, smiling at T. while her eyes filled with tears.

Drinking and eating, they changed their positions at Sophia's behest, to form new conversational groupings. At some point word got around that Olga was going on the boat with T.; Sophia, hearing that, could almost believe T.'s journey to be an extended version of one of her own weekends: in any event, it helped to make his trip human, understandable. . . . One by one, the travelers began to doze. Dr. Kuvshinnikov, wakened by thunder or perhaps the vibration of the still-open door as the train went over a road crossing at some godforsaken hamlet, found that Sophia and Isaac along with others had gone to the next compartment; seated opposite him, next to the snoring Olga, was Lika, apparently awake—her posture suggested that—but with her eyes closed. Her hair was gleaming in the dim glow of the oil lamp on the wall. T. was standing, alone, in the corridor, staring into the compartment. Was he looking with such longing at the beautiful Lika? But his eyes seemed focused more toward the window. Dr. Kuvshinnikov turned to look at whatever T. was seeing. In the blackness he saw the light of a tavern; in a flash of lightning, the steeple of a church, and beyond it a pale landscape that stretched on to become one with the sky. The edges of the clouds on the horizon were glowing as if from a fire hidden deeply within them. Then the rain began to beat against the window, distorting whatever was to be seen; and Dr. Kuvshinnikov—not hearing the repeated coughing, muffled as it was by a bloody handkerchief— closed his eyes and slept as peacefully as the others.

5

In his fiftieth year, T.'s father, hiding beneath a straw mat to escape detection by his creditors, slipped out of town in a cart and boarded the train for Moscow at a waystation. In Moscow Paul found a job as a police clerk, but soon lost it through incompetency. During those years in which T. remained behind in his native town to finish his high school education, Paul and Eugenia and their other children moved from one small and damp apartment to the next; often they were without wood for the stove or food for the next meal. Having nothing left but his despotism as a salvage for his honor, Paul fastened to the wall a schedule of duties for the children that even included what they were to do with their "free" time; and at the bottom of the list he wrote, "Failure to fulfill these duties will result first in a stern reprimand, then in punishment during which it is forbidden to cry." In much the manner of the

commanding general of a division or an army, he signed his
orders with his name and authority ("Father of the Family").

Bullying is always an admission of defeat, and Paul
must have been desperately aware of his own when, having
altered the schedule by advancing the hour of eleven-year-
old Michael's awakening after the boy was asleep, he punished him the next morning for not getting up on time; or
when he gave such a fierce beating to Ivan that the youth
screamed, whatever the regulation against outcries, causing
the neighbors to complain to the landlord of the noise.
Improbable or Dickensian as such behavior may seem,
even the more rigorous of the recent biographers accepts
the general details as true—although not Alexander's em-
bellishments of them (comedy perhaps being his only way
of communicating the pathos and degradation) in his letters
to T., letters that also said their mother was demoralized
and ebbing away while their sister was constantly crying.

Years later, after his return from Sakhalin, T. went
deeply into debt in order to buy a country estate for himself and his family. It permitted him to live away from
Moscow, and yet was close enough so that Mary, who
taught in the city, could visit on weekends as well as live
there (as did Ivan) during the summer vacation. Michael,
the tax official, was able to arrange a transfer to the neigh-
borhood, and moved permanently to the villa. And Paul
and Eugenia were established there, of course.

Long before his journey, T. had been a guest at a
number of country estates and had admired their ball-
rooms, parks, gardens, and serene vistas. Undoubtedly,
whatever guilt he might have felt for giving up the rented
house on Sadovaya-Kudrinskaya Street was mitigated by
his dream of a grander home for himself and his family. So
strong was his desire for splendid isolation—for a villa with
ponds and a stream and forests and fertile farmland—that
he contracted to buy his, sight unseen, as soon as the prop-

erty became available; he had lost an earlier estate through caution and delays beyond his control. But it turned out that this estate had been misrepresented to him. After the snow had melted sufficiently to reveal what he had bought, he found an alley of lindens and a gazebo; he also discovered that the forests had been cut for timber, the vistas were dull, the stream was a "mangy" one, the outbuildings and fences were dilapidated, and the house itself was without a toilet and infested with vermin. Each of the ten small rooms was in need of extensive renovation, and even the well was inadequate. (Lack of sufficient water for washing and drinking is a problem too remote for an American city dweller to comprehend. Twenty-odd years ago—back far enough in time that T. was just becoming of major interest to me—I moved with my family to a farmhouse in a much better state of repair than his, but on our first night the well went dry; I felt so depressed I couldn't sleep, for the expected liberation of a country existence seemed but a snare, a trap for the guileless.)

Still, reality did not destroy T.'s optimism. With considerable enthusiasm, he undertook that first spring and summer of his occupancy the task of making the house more habitable and its surroundings more park-like and productive. What interests me, though, is the degree to which the family, under his direction, came to reflect the disciplined life that Paul had tried to impose on them in the years of their privation in Moscow, and which T. to his dismay observed during his infrequent visits while he was still a high school student. Although laborers were hired to remodel the house, T. and the other family members worked longer hours than any of them. With the family's concurrence, T. instituted a daily schedule much as his father had done; everybody rose at dawn, and each had his or her assigned duties—Eugenia the household chores, Paul the task of clearing old garden paths and constructing new ones, Mary the responsibility for the planting and tending of vegetables in their large plot, Michael for plow-

ing and seeding the farmland, and T. himself the pruning
and general revitalization of the orchard and the planting of
bushes and bulbs. T. also made the decisions on important
matters such as the placement of a new well and a larger
pond; and as soon as he possibly could, he began setting
out new trees that would become imposing, as pine woods
or cherry orchard, only after his death. Like all agricultural
workers, the family members went to bed early, and slept
so soundly that they weren't awakened by the shouts and
cries or the pervasive smell of smoke on the night the house
of their nearest neighbor burned.

It is no wonder that within such an environment Paul
mellowed, reserving his old authoritarianism for certain of
the hired help whenever T. wasn't present. Paul's life has
an unusual symmetry to it. The house—the *family* house,
since all of them had contributed their labor to it—was,
with the completion of the remodeling, finer than the one
he had lost, and in it he could once again lead his children
in singing the traditional hymns. Indeed, at Easter, he
served again as choirmaster, for the church in the nearest
village. After the daily chores were completed, there was
time—until the family members could no longer keep their
eyes open—for conversation and reading; and later, when
they were in their beds, T. and the others could hear Paul
praying before the ikon in his bedroom and softly chanting
the church rituals.

A son's choice of real estate and spiritual attitudes—
the two are not so distinct as they might seem—has something to do with his observation of his father's dreams,
losses, and convictions. A desire to be other than the father
is particularly strong if that parent is domineering and conscious of his status; but no son, however much he would
like to reject his father's values, can do much more than
make a displacement of them, one that (if he is fortunate)
spills the waters over a kindlier and more productive soil.
In his early months in the country, T. referred to himself in
letters as "landowner" and as possessor of "a ducal estate,"

terms whereby he could channel and laugh at his own pretensions to a status that, purified by mockery, could
gratify him.

As for religious attitudes, he would seem at first
glance to have separated himself completely from his
father. He had long since renounced Paul's orthodoxy,
finding in it the same authoritarianism that had charac-
terized his father's treatment of wife and children. Even
toward the end of his life, T. was still declaring his bewil-
derment that any person of intelligence could say he or she
was a believer; in any of its contemporary tendencies or
aberrations, Christianity was no more than "a survival,
already the end of what is dying or dead." Maybe "tens of
thousands of years hence"—an example of T.'s continued
trust in human progress, however slow the movement toward the millenium—"Mankind may know the true, real
God," but not now, not here. And yet his years in the
country demonstrate more clearly than any other period of
his life his adherence to a basic Christian injunction. Desiring separation from the city and its gossip, he nevertheless
wished to share his new life with old friends, and invited
them to come from Moscow or Petersburg for visits that
his hospitality often made lengthy; needing time for his
writing, he nevertheless established a clinic in his home,
where he gave medical advice and treatment to peasants
unable to pay for his services with anything more than a
few potatoes. In addition, he worked to obtain the schools
and education necessary before the peasant children could
overcome the ignorance, frequent brutality, and poverty of
their parents. Whatever his flaws (his father often irritated
him, he sometimes quarreled with those he most loved,
and he came to accept as a given Mary's devotion to his
career and well-being), T. in his human relationships was a
far better Christian than Paul.

He lived in the country for six years, and regardless of
his complaints of boredom, they constituted the most idyl-
lic span of his brief life. He sold the estate only after his

father had died and his own deteriorating health required him to find a milder climate. So far as his fiction was concerned, those years were rich, despite the demands on his time; and the finest story of that rural period came at the very end of it.

This story is one of three told, in turn, by three acquaintances—a teacher, Burkin; a veterinarian, Ivan Ivanych; and an overworked and lonely owner of an estate, Alyohin. All three stories present variations of T.'s most constant literary theme, the restrictions we consciously or unconsciously impose upon the degree of freedom and happiness possible for us; but in this grandest story of the three, which is the one told by Ivan, we are given a completely happy man—Ivan's brother, Nicholas. Ivan relates to his two acquaintances the account of a visit he once paid to Nicholas at the estate his brother had finally purchased (in some respects the description of it is that of T.'s own estate, as it looked on the day he first saw it; and it is likely that T. planted some gooseberry bushes, for his estate had some, even as Nicholas did as one of his first acts) after a lifetime of struggling for such a dream. To obtain the property, the brother had been mean-spirited and obsequious; he married an elderly and unattractive widow for her money, and hastened her death through his stinginess, lack of affection, and neglect. But now the brother, a former clerk, was lawgiver to his village, the peasants bowed before him, and he had even concocted an aristocratic lineage for himself. Fat and content as a pig, he lived wholly within the illusions not only of his lineage, but of the wisdom and compassion of his treatment of the peasants, the beauty of his estate, and the sweetness of his gooseberries. Ivan says he tasted one, finding it sour. As a consequence of this visit, he tells his friends, his life has been changed; never again can he, himself, be happy or content. The world is full of such injustice and pain and so many malnourished or starving children that complacency is intolerable, and happiness a condition of stupidity or arrogance possible only because those who suffer do so silently.

In the most famous passage of the narrative, the passionate Ivan declares, "Behind the door of every contented, happy man there ought to be someone standing with a little hammer and continually reminding him with a knock that there are unhappy people, that however happy he may be, life will sooner or later show him its claws, and trouble will come to him—illness, poverty, losses, and then no one will see or hear him, just as now he neither sees nor hears others"; and, pacing up and down the room, he bemoans the fact of his advanced age, his personal inability to redeem the world. Of his friends, he implores, "There is no happiness and there should be none, and if life has a meaning and a purpose, that meaning and purpose is not our happiness but something greater and more rational. Do good!" Soon thereafter, having transferred the burden to the others, he falls asleep—though Burkin lies long awake, bothered by the smell of stale tobacco coming from Ivan's pipe.

The frame that T. constructs for Ivan's gloomy tale about happiness—a tale his friends don't particularly want to hear—is a hunting trip undertaken by Ivan and Burkin. They have been tramping about the countryside on a sultry day, apparently shooting in the random and harmless manner of most of T.'s gun-bearing characters, and arrive at Alyohin's estate during a downpour, soaked and irritable. While Alyohin, who is covered with dust and grime from the threshing, washes himself in the millpond, Burkin and Ivan go for a swim in the rain, and Ivan in particular has a glorious time of it—" 'By God!' he kept repeating delightedly, 'by God!' " as he comes up from yet another dive to the bottom—; and it is after this swim that Ivan tells his story, amid the splendor of the busy Alyohin's normally unused drawing room on the upper floor. All three of the friends are dressed in comfortable slippers and luxurious robes and are consuming tea and preserves brought to them

by a servant so lovely her prototype in real life might well
have been the beautiful Lika.

To what extent is Ivan's outburst against happiness a
result of his guilt for his own sensuous pleasure? The
ironies resonate against the walls not only of the story's
chamber, but of the one that contains its creator. In a way,
the entire story seems an elegy to a lost dream of happiness—a fantasy of what country living can afford. No
estate could provide undiluted happiness to anybody who
had made T.'s displacement of a parent's values, as on
some level he must have realized even as he was purchasing
his. Whatever the exaggerations in portraiture, the characters of both Ivan and his brother reflect antithetical qualities which T., that most objective of writers, perceived as
undesirable in himself; one led him to value things of this
world unduly, the other to reject them as worthless. In
terms of the religion he had renounced, those opposing
urges come from the body and the soul. Each in its own
way is myopic and narcissistic. Surely the Ivan in T. is far
stronger than the Nicholas; but what intrigues me in this
post-Sakhalin story is T.'s awareness that an embittered
and abstract desire for justice and goodness—for an absolute so distinct from the humanity whose woes it seemingly
would redress that it would prevent individuals from ob-
taining any possible joy—can be as selfish as an appetite for
material goods.

I should admit that for years my own emotional
identification with Ivan was intense enough that I didn't
realize the degree to which T., without ostensibly doing
so, passes judgment on him even as Ivan is passing judgment on Nicholas. Such impartiality is remarkable in an
author who is delineating a character with whom he shares
a psychic bond. As a medical practitioner who at last must
have been fully aware of what his physical symptoms
prophesied, T. had to be personally aware of the waiting
claws he has his doctor of animals almost vengefully mention in that diatribe against happiness. And in a story full

of deeply-felt but often questionable exhortations, T. is, I think, almost one with Ivan when he has him say, "To retire from the city, from the struggle, from the hubbub, to go off and hide on one's own farm—that's not life, it is selfishness, sloth, it is a kind of monasticism, but monasticism without works. Man needs not six feet of earth, not a farm, but the whole globe, all of Nature, where unhindered he can display all the capacities and peculiarities of his free spirit."

Having buried his father, written this story, and departed from his estate, T. settled in a seaside resort with a climate that attracted many who, like him, were consumptive. He bought a parcel of land with a distant view of the sea, and hired a young architect to help him plan the house he would build; Mary and he decided on the placement of the flowering shrubs, the orchard, and the flower and vegetable gardens in the barren and limited space available. While the house was being constructed, he bought, on impulse, a picturesque cottage that had a much more encompassing view of sky and water and land, but was remote from town and difficult to reach, since it was on the crest of a steep hill. Neither place satisfied him; he thought of supplementing them with a strip of property on the sea, one with a beach for swimming—although such exercise was now beyond his strength. And whatever the drawbacks of city living, he longed for a dwelling in Moscow. These conflicts over real estate are conflicts of an Ivan who never will be at peace with his brother.

Can one accept, and find purpose in, the essence of a religion while discarding its framework? A staunch believer in any religion—a convert to Catholicism, for example, who has known the struggle for acceptance and submission and now lives with the possibility of miraculous grace—would say no, and would find in T.'s lifelong struggle for an impossible freedom the desire of a soul permanently exiled from its true home. T. himself would say no, for he felt that the lack of faith and the concomitant inability to know truth constituted not only his major handicap but that of his age. Throughout his life, he also insisted that a writer's job is to present the questions and not the answers, and that his lack of solutions was neither a moral nor an artistic flaw; and yet a story like the one about Ivan and Nicholas, which finally resonates beyond any conceivable room or antithesis, implies the possibility of a grace-bearing answer, however temporal—even evanescent—it may be. Perhaps the two largest ironies of T.'s life and work are that the very rigor of his literary objectivity gives the distance which permits intimate revelations he would hide even from himself; and that in the greatest adventure of his life, the journey to Sakhalin, he personally acts out the truth embedded in his creative work, and hence merges into the very fabric of his stories and plays. If "all of Nature" excludes mankind, it as well as a plot of ground becomes an escape, the "monasticism without works" of an embittered soul; and it is lucky for T. that his journey into a vast and empty landscape had for its goal a human colony.

6

———

Olga Kundasov, at once the most impulsive and intelligent of T.'s friends, looked with care at whatever of his writings came her way. Dutifully, she read his stories in the manner in which she knew he wanted her to—that is, as artistic entities which, however much they might be based on personal observation and experience, were resolutely free of subjective bias, the observation having the disinterestedness of science—and yet (as the friend of any writer inevitably does, especially one whose mind has a keen analytical edge) she examined them again for what they revealed about him. Recently, much as if she were a clairvoyant and his work the globe into which she peered, she had seen a cloudy mass that disquieted her. This was the reason, or part of it, that she had decided to accompany him for a few days on the river. To Lika she had implied that T. knew nothing of her decision, but this was not quite true—she had told that near-lie for the other's sake,

47

knowing that Lika was extraordinarily fond of T. On the previous day, visiting at the house while T. was frantically trying to remember everything he had forgotten to buy for his expedition, she asked him if he thought tickets for his steamer could be purchased at the dock. "Do you want to come with me?" he asked, surprised by such a question. "Yes," she said; and he simply laughed in response, before rushing off to buy several pairs of warm socks.

It was like T. to wait until the last moment for such a necessary purchase, and also like him to behave as if she were making a joke: this meant she could come if she wished to, but did not tell her whether he would be pleased or vexed. Whenever they weren't reflecting pleasure, and sometimes even then, T.'s eyes seemed to hold an understanding of life in all its painful complexities, a quality that was chiefly responsible for the feelings he aroused in women, especially in girls as idealistic and innocent as Lika; but despite his obvious caring for people in their suffering, he himself preferred to skate on the slippery surface of human relationships, like a benign monk whose tolerance to small sins was part of his charm. Indeed, dozing in the train, she dreamed of T. as skating across a frozen lake so immense it curved with the horizon, his priestly robes flapping behind him; he was wearing his pince-nez, for he was reading an illuminated manuscript while munching on a piece of salami. The image, which carried her affection for him, was so ludicrous that she laughed aloud, the guffaw sending him flying away and waking her.

Oh, her detestable barks of laughter, her bizarre shrieks of amazement, her uncontrollable pokings into another's rib with her elbow! She would have resisted such responses if she could; but her continual surprise at the strangeness of life got in her way. She couldn't even take her own amatory experiences seriously; however reckless, cheerful, and warm-hearted she seemed, she was dissatisfied and felt somehow separate from experience.

Perhaps Olga, had she lived in a world of true sexual equality, would not have found her intelligence quite the alienating force it was; perhaps in such a world she would have been free of her annoying spasms and tics and of her need for outlandish clothes, and would have moderated her espousal of free love and anarchy without compromising her belief in social and political liberty. Like T., it was freedom she wanted; but her sex made an adventure like his, one that would take him at least temporarily beyond the constraints of civilization, impossible. T. was her sole acquaintance, male or female, who delighted in her intellectual abilities, finding in them no sexual threat. She could, at least, accompany him for a brief distance—and perhaps be of that kind of help which affection itself, even if it is wordless, can bring.

Not only Olga, but a few other acquaintances and several critics of the kind he despised, found suggestions of despair in T.'s most recent long piece of fiction. It angered him that others would see in his objective account of an anguished and sardonic soul—one that hovered between nostalgia and bitterness—a revelation of his personal feelings about meaninglessness. His fictional character, a professor of medicine at Moscow University, was, after all, more than twice his age, a man near death from an unspecified, self-diagnosed illness. The professor is a celebrity, famous throughout Europe for his scientific writings; but as his death approaches, he becomes ever more aware that his life is devoid of any controlling idea. Tolstoy, the most revered of the older generation of Russian writers, had written of a somewhat similar, if less intellectual, figure who in his dying moments finds his meaning in the self-renunciation of a spiritual acceptance; but T. carried his story to a conclusion more consistent with his character's temperament and habits. He had given to his dying man (or so it seemed to Olga) the helpless fear of emptiness he had felt ever since the death from consumption of his brother Nicholas.

The kinship between T. and his character seemed unmistakable. To the professor of medicine T. had imparted his own distaste for a fame that defined him as other than he was, that prevented others from treating him as simply another human being; he had given his character his own financial worries, and the same ironic awareness of the difference between reputation and monetary reward. Olga could hear T. talking in his own voice when he had the professor write in his journal about freedom and literature and the state of the theater—and especially when he had the professor affirm "that learning is the most important, splendid and vital thing in man's life, that it always has been and always will be the highest manifestation of love, and that it alone can enable man to conquer nature and himself."

But why wasn't that enough? Why did that brave affirmation give Olga a joy when she first came across the words and then such a profound sadness for him that it reached out to include herself as well? Sometimes, to tease T., who tried too strenuously to divorce himself from the ideological currents of the age, she told him that everything in his art was a consequence of events surrounding his birth—not only the Great Reforms, but the publication of such works as Darwin's *Origin of Species* and Buckle's *History of Civilization*, as well as the death of Schopenhauer, which brought (as the deaths of eminent people with difficult personalities sometimes do) a belated appreciation of his ideas. If Darwin unwittingly had undermined tenets of a traditional religious faith through patient observation and scientific theory, Buckle had simultaneously provided a new faith (and faith it was, since the statistical methods of *his* science of history were atrocious) in the slow, perhaps crablike, movement of mankind toward a greater perfectibility—thus granting optimism to the evolutionary hypothesis. Buckle believed in the influence of geography on what he considered the antithetical qualities of imagination and understanding. More importantly, he believed that the efforts of individuals are inconsequential, heroes or other dominant figures serving as but the expression of the underlying spirit of their time; and that progress consists of the knowledge gained by mankind as a whole, and is a consequence of a skepticism that routs credulity and thus the religious superstitions of the imagination.

Schopenhauer was another matter. Olga thought the new or renewed interest in him a consequence of his dogged and skeptical concern with spiritual questions that science by its very nature had to ignore. He was obsessed by the conception of reality as an impelling and blind force that in man becomes the incredible will to live—a will that creates dissatisfaction and pain from its unsatiated desires, and yet, in its moral manifestation, enables the individual to sympathize with others and to attempt to alleviate that general suffering which is identical with his own. Questing for its unobtainable pleasure, the will finds momentary rest in ennui and ultimate liberation in mystical acceptance. To Olga, such a philosophy was a kind of intellectual surgery performed on religion long before anybody had heard of Darwin or Buckle, but which required them in order to become respectable. By cutting away the authority and miracles and ceremony of dogma, that surgery exposed the secrets of the pulsating heart; it was a cruel examination of the spiritual impulse itself, the divinity and hope with which Christianity had covered it being stripped away like impeding flesh.

Some months before the publication of his story about the dying professor, Olga told T. that he believed at once in a splendid future made possible through incremental growth in knowledge and in the resignation and detachment of Nirvana. "No wonder, Anton, you're so popular with readers," she said, a remark rendered harmless by her whoops of glee. And yet perhaps that story confirmed much of what she'd said. Wasn't the professor's affirmation of the value of learning a reflection both of T.'s trust in human progress and of his personal separation from life? Love to character and author alike was an abstraction that had nothing to do with the embrace of one human being by another. But possibly Olga herself, concerned as she was with the nature of reality (the mind, contemplating that question, finds itself unreal and abstract) and ideological currents of the age (the present being the bobbing twig in an uncontrollable stream of ideas and events), was simply another desperate example of loneliness and unanswerable questions; if that were the case, then possibly one could say that T., in examining his own psyche, was examining that of an age, and hence was being scientific and impersonal after all. . . .

Aboard the train, though, how excited and talkative she was, jabbering away to Lika and the others, happy in her thoughts of traveling with T. on the steamer! But would T. remember her "Yes" to his question about her wish to accompany him? Preoccupied as he was, his laugh might have meant only the dismissal from his memory of a bothersome request. The rain poured down during the last half of the trip. Like the others, Olga slept, but was frequently awakened by the intensity of her dreams and the melancholy engine whistle. Briefly, the raindrops turned to sleet, like white grains of sand flying horizontally past the window. They might have been traversing some Sahara, an illusion of tropical heat made possible by the coziness of the carriage, whose warmth was provided by the packed bodies. The sleeping occupants held each other up: Olga herself, leaning against the window, was supporting Lika, whose hair was a golden waterfall streaming down Olga's own breasts, as if she had been transformed from a frog or clumsy beast into the maiden of a fairy story. A possibility, an abstract ideal out of her dreams, took possession of her like a reality, as her mind hovered on the edge of sleep, that magical borderland between two equally strange worlds.

At the Yaroslavl terminus, a dreary and damp building, she slipped away, hiding her satchel as best she could within the folds of her coat, while T. was embracing his family members and friends and accepting from Dr. Kuvshinnikov a leather pouch filled with brandy to drink only after he reached the edge of the continent. Thunder rolled over the rooftops as she ran toward the pier through the rain. The ship was an enchanting castle of twinkling lights to be reached by a wooden drawbridge over its fish-smelling moat. But first one had to stop at a little booth to purchase a ticket (hers the cheapest, without accommodations, to a town several days down the Volga.) She stood in the main cabin at a window overlooking the gangway.

Finally T. appeared, his leather coat glistening in the rain. Behind him came a carriage driver, carrying T.'s largest piece of luggage; and behind him, a young man with two smaller bags. The carriage driver left as soon as he was paid; the young man, who wore no raincoat, was as wet as Olga herself, but remained on board. He was obviously an admirer of T., overcome with joy at his luck in meeting him at the station; he kept bowing and pointing to the luggage. T. ignored him as best he could, looking helplessly up and down the deck. Could he be trying to find her? Why didn't she reveal herself? When T. came toward the cabin door, she slipped into the shadows. She felt at once exalted and shy—as shy, even, as the beautiful Lika. She remained concealed while the young admirer helped T. carry all the luggage to his stateroom; only after the man was gone and T. was standing on the deck, peering through the dark at the pier and the booth, did she come out.

"Olga!" he cried, embracing her. "Thank God! Come, you're soaked," and he took her hand, briskly pulling her through the door and down the corridor, exclaiming that he thought she had become lost or been murdered—Yaroslavl was a beastly and sinister town, full of mud and lurking human shapes, and even the advertisements on the buildings and in the station were ugly and full of misspellings. He led her into a small room crowded by his luggage. There were two bunks, one above the other, a

chair, a washstand with mirror and towel rack, a ward-
robe, and a porthole. He embraced her again. "You're
cold, Olga! Why, you're shivering! You must get out of
your clothes. But first, drink this," and he handed her the
leather pouch of brandy that, as she had left the station, she
had heard Dr. Kuvshinnikov tell him to drink after he saw
the ocean.

"Wouldn't it bring bad luck to drink it now?"

"Come, Olga! We're educated and reasonable."

"Even an atheist like me can cling to a superstition or
two."

"I don't! The oratory that came with this little gift
made me want to drink it then and there." But he was
looking doubtfully at the pouch. "Perhaps, from con-
sideration of the donor . . ." Laughing, he grabbed back
the pouch, and gave her instead a half-empty bottle of
brandy that had been buried in flannel shirts in one of his
bags.

"To the triumph of reason," she said, taking a mouth-
ful of brandy as he began to massage her dripping hair with
a towel. Oh, but her new and unreasonable and even child-
like shyness! She and T. were modern people; they disre-
garded convention and platitudes. Still, her face burned
with more than brandy as she turned her back to him and
slipped off her dress and underwear and shrugged into her
long nightgown. She stood before the mirror to attend to
her hair, which came down in tangled strands over her
eyes. As she brushed them back, her eyes stared at her
from the mirror, shining and timorous and so unfamiliar
that she almost cried out.

Meanwhile, T. had not stopped talking; in his excitement, he was as much a geyser as Dr. Kuvshinnikov. He
was behaving toward her as he always did, as a friend to
whom he could say whatever he wished. He was speaking
of a disagreeable experience on the train; she'd been in the
other compartment, and would never know his suffering.
And to think that, upon escaping from the train, he would

at once be accosted by a young admirer who wanted to become a writer and who kept repeating his own name so that T. would remember it and someday put in a word for him!

"One smiles and nods," T. said. "But every gesture, every word, one makes in return is a kind of subterfuge. We have within us a sense of our identity—a knowledge of what we are and a purity of soul sufficient to let us know what we ought to be. Maybe this secret identity doesn't exist, maybe it's a lie—who's to say?—and yet through it we know ourselves; it's what we respond to when people call us by name, 'Olga,' 'Anton.' But how difficult it is to conceive of any ideal against which we can define our nature when these same people keep on talking and we must nod yes or no or defend ourselves against some falsehood or shield ourselves from malice or flattery."

And he, himself, kept on talking, asking her if this was not so, as he paced the tiny room, stumbling now and then against his luggage. He was as emotional, as inconsistent, and finally as self-serving, as any of his own characters. By this time, Olga was sitting in the chair; as T. sank onto the lower bunk, he banged his head against the upper one. Their knees almost touched. Normally Olga would have responded to his state of nerves by laughing uproariously, poking him, or demonstrating the flaws of his argument; but normally she wouldn't be with him on a boat, wearing a nightgown. It was enough that he was glad she was there, as a comrade in his struggle against hostile forces. There was a rattle of chains; the floor throbbed. Through the porthole she could see a light drifting past. She still was living in the borderland that was magical and yet real; everything she had experienced or dreamed became, in comparison, alien and bizarre. "Anton?" she asked tentatively, in the midst of his discourse; the movement of the ship, the sense of the people left behind, had given her a thought.

"Yes?"

"What's your opinion of the Beguny?"

"The Beguny?" Her question was such a non sequitur that he was bewildered; it was as if he had just been awakened from a world in which he had been lecturing on a subject without substance. "The Beguny believe they find God in solitude, don't they? A strange sect. That's all I know."

"Yes; a sect of our own Russian people who find God in separating themselves from others, by losing themselves in the steppes and mountains." Her voice was so quiet and meditative, so tender, that it belonged to another, to Mary or Lika. "Buckle, you see, was right: our landscapes are boundless, and so also our spiritual desires. Maybe all of us belong to that sect to one degree or another, even though we have no religion, but you more than most. The wish to be that kind of wanderer runs through your stories, a spiritual thread, and you can't—" for he had begun to object— "you can't deny it by calling your work 'impersonal' or 'scientific.'"

The boat whistle sounded its raspy cry, merging with her memory of the locomotive whistle that earlier in the night had roused her from dreams. T. was looking at her in astonishment. Was it that her voice was lower than usual, and carried so easily the burden of her love for him, her anxiety and caring? Her facial tics, her horsey whinnyings and doggy barks, had vanished. "I don't pretend to know everything in your soul, Anton, or what possesses you to leave those who love you far behind; but I know there is danger in what you're doing. Sometimes, at the observatory, when I was lonely and dissatisfied with my life, I would look through the telescope at a star, and it was as if my soul swooshed up through that empty metal tube, going up and up like a speck of dust, and I felt such a painful joy that the star blurred and danced about—a pure jewel, impersonal and burning. If somebody spoke to me, his voice seemed depraved, a horror, no matter how kind the words; and I would be ashamed of myself. 'Come, come,'

I would say to myself. 'You are Olga Kundasov, you are a mathematician, get back to your statistics'; and God knows there is pleasure in that, figures are comfortable, they make rational sense."

T. continued to look at her in wonder. He reached forward to stroke her head. "Really, Olga, you should keep your hair damp and straight like this, it suits your cheekbones."

She took his hand in her own. "We may not be believers, Anton, but we are spiritual wanderers nevertheless, and need a Christ, somebody of flesh and blood, to bring us back to mankind, to teach us through humility and example to devote ourselves—to give ourselves—to others." Was this invocation of their lost religion simply an appeal for a wholly human contact, a sensual love? Regardless, Olga felt she spoke the truth, and looked steadily into T.'s eyes while still holding his hand.

T. looked as steadily back. "Why, Olga, how beautiful you are!" he exclaimed in delight. Had he heard a word she'd said? He kissed her on the forehead, and sprang to his feet, ducking his head just in time to miss the upper bunk. "But what nonsense you speak! To find God—yes, that would be a frightening sensation, I would be terrified, I would throw my arms around the next person I saw. But I've never had a divine revelation and never shall, maybe that's my trouble. My life is as aimless and random as anybody's. . . . At night, if a man gets restless, he takes his dog for a walk: walking a dog gives him purpose, as everybody understands who peers out a window to see him. When the dog lifts his leg against a tree, the man and his walk are justified. If it is daylight and he has this same restless urge even though it may be raining, he takes a gun and a dog and goes into the woods—a bird or a rabbit, whether he shoots one or not, gives him the same justification. Tomorrow, when you and I have breakfast in the dining room, people will look at you, particularly if your hair is wet—" he laughed, pleased by his teasing

"—and will say 'How beautiful she is!' and will think about why we shared a room and are taking a lazy trip on a river. After you leave me, what then? I will be desolate, of course. But if strangers ask me, I will say firmly, 'I am going to Sakhalin, an island thousands of miles away, to investigate the conditions there.' That sentence will satisfy strangers as it will satisfy me. I am taking a trip to have a goal in my life, it's as simple as that."

He was talking as rapidly, and laughing as much, as had Olga on the train, or as she did at any party; and it was obvious to her that the very sexual attractiveness and womanly modesty he had found in her was putting him at a distance from her, that if she were as beautiful as Lika he would never have permitted her to come, and that their long comradeship with its degree of intimacy was based upon two indisputable facts: that she really was not beautiful and that the two of them were temperamentally unfitted for an enduring attachment or even an overnight romance. He needed to be as free of her as she of him.

During the night, she heard him cry out once in the bunk above her, clamber down, and stumble about the room. The floor was vibrating, so the boat was still moving, but the porthole was as dark as the room itself. "What's the matter, Anton?" she asked, sitting up.

"I'm looking for my bottle of brandy. Ah, here it is." He sat beside her; she could hear the liquid gurgle from the bottle as he drank. "Do you want some?" he asked.

"Why not?" And she too drank.

"I had a nightmare. I've had it before."

"What was it?"

"The black head of an animal. A bull, I think."

"Why is that so frightening?"

"I don't know. It doesn't have any eyes. Sometimes it gets so large it fills the room. But it's the blindness, the lack of eyes."

"Poor darling."

"The bull?"

"You."

Then he curled up beside her, on the narrow bunk; and for the rest of the night they turned one way or the other, uncomfortable but content in their embrace.

At breakfast the next morning, Olga attracted the attention of the other diners with the loudness of her laugh and her extravagant gestures. The sun came out, and so they sat together on deck, watching the shore; and they joked and teased each other. That night they slept in their separate bunks. On the following morning, long before Olga woke, T. went into the lounge to write a letter to Mary and the other members of the family. He wrote about what he had seen from the boat—the white churches gleaming in the sunshine, the monasteries, the water meadows, the wideness of the river. And, because he knew they would be wondering about Olga, he added that she was traveling with him. "Where she is going and with what object I don't know," he wrote.

When I question her about it, she launches off into extremely misty allusions about someone who has appointed a tryst with her in a ravine near Kineshma, then goes off into a wild giggle and begins stamping her feet or prodding with her elbow whatever comes first. We have passed both Kineshma and the ravine, but she still goes on in the steamer, at which of course I am very much pleased; by the way, yesterday for the first time in my life I saw her eating. She eats no less than other people, but she eats mechanically, as though she were munching oats.

Was he writing her off, with these words? The caricature, if that is what it is, contains the affection we have for one who is soon to leave us; watching her leave the ship that evening, T. was depressed and lonely.

7

The year I spent in Florence with my family was the happiest I have known, but it didn't start out that way. Although I had escaped my country, I hadn't my past: I had yet to overcome the fatigue and spiritual paralysis brought by the previous year of near-chaos on my university campus—protest meetings, marches, building take-overs, arson, isolated acts of brutality, the threat of guns in a racial confrontation.

In retrospect, that year of demands and violence becomes a banality, as does any major human drift into separate and destructive camps. Given the distance of space or time, war is such a banality, for victor and vanquished alike; and so is the stockpiling of nuclear weapons by two or more nations, each of which says it has no other choice. We are a single species with a single life, and if we bring upon ourselves the Apocalypse we will cover every creative and gracious act we ever have managed—all of the documented and the infinite number of unheralded instances of kindness and generosity and love from the beginning of history; the scientific discoveries and artistic achievements, including T.'s stories and plays—with the same banal shroud that already covers Hitler and Attila the Hun.

"Do good!" Ivan the veterinarian implores; he and the professor of medicine and many other of T.'s central characters speak with the mingled idealism and despair that my accents might seem but to imitate. Talking from the heart is a normal activity for them—it is, after all, part of their cultural heritage. As a teacher of literature, I try to express in seminars my personal response to a text, and sometimes I wonder—so foreign to us is this attempt to speak of our deepest feelings—if I don't sound deranged. But discourse of this sort is so customary in the society that T. writes about that his characters will confess that their revelations are boring or dreary—and then cheerfully go on with their philosophizing, and with those stories that carry the burden of their most troubling emotions. T. uses their idealism (indistinguishable, it often seems, from his own) as a means of understanding not so much their strengths as their flaws and weaknesses: despite his apparent scientific objectivity, his psychology has more of a spiritual than a clinical ring to it, his characters being tested against the purity of the most precious metal instead of a common and debased currency.

Partial or faulty as it may be, my present insight into T.'s nature and work permits me to see myself—not only as I was during that year of intense campus disturbance but in those preparatory years that gave to brutal confrontation its excuse, its aura of inevitability—as a character he might have created. It was a time, God knows, in which Americans, particularly those in university communities, did talk openly of what was on their minds and in their hearts. Call me Jimski, a romantic by temperament, a believer in the spiritual equality of all human beings; a person who could speak, sometimes eloquently and sometimes not, about novels and plays and poems, but one who always felt that in raising his voice to lecture on a novel to an auditorium of students he was, in a sense, engaged in a lie—that is, was transforming by the volume and rhetorical nature of his voice certain subjective evaluations into objective facts and fixed principles. I told my students not to take notes on what I was saying, and certainly not to give back to me on examinations and term papers a garbled version of my views, but rather to present their own considered responses: I asked them to trust themselves, to listen to their inner voices.

In *War and Peace*, Tolstoy appropriated Buckle's belief in the overshadowing of heroes by social forces in order to make Napoleon a puppet of his times. Tolstoy later renounced his version of Buckle's theory, as well as the entirety of the grand novel containing it, but that theory has validity for the American sixties. A general, slowly-growing revulsion against our activities in Vietnam created an idealistic upsurge—a spouting, like that from a nearly-submerged whale—which held aloft, first on college campuses and then elsewhere, a series of new leaders, some old but mainly young, some honorable and others not, all of whom were attacking whatever was capricious, hypocritical, and discriminatory in our institutions and assumptions.

My pedagogical attitudes were congenial to the period. During those difficult years, I took pride in my perception that my students cared more deeply than ever for the old verities of books. In the midst of meetings and demonstrations, attendance in my classes, always voluntary, had never been so high. With many others, I saw my students' idealism as a fragile and lovely quality that held whatever hope for the future we had. I felt for those students much of the protective love I felt for my own sons, two of whom were facing perplexing questions about the draft and might yet be maimed, spiritually and physically, by a confused and violent world.

One incident stands out as emblematic of my responses. With a colleague and three of our students, all young women, I attended an anti–Vietnam War demonstration in Washington; through a mix-up in arrangements, we spent the preceding night sleeping in our clothes in a child's playhouse in the yard of a Maryland country estate—the five of us on a gym mat with a musty carpet for cover. Perhaps in part because my father had always introduced me to his acquaintances as "doctor" or "professor," I have never liked titles, or anything that distinguishes individuals by giving them a niche in a hierarchy; in any event, the communal nature of both the march and our accommodations gave me happiness.

It would be tiresome to chronicle all the events that led me as close to a breakdown as I expect I'll ever come. Like Ivan, I'm much better at exhorting others to do good than I am at doing it myself; but for a brief time I had the illusion that I was helping to heal the sores of social divisiveness. I joined some of my colleagues in forming the faculty of a free evening school whose aim was to provide a basic education for the poor of our community; and, after the assassination of Martin Luther King, participated in organizing a group devoted to helping minorities find jobs and decent housing. Perhaps because of these activities, I was elected to the faculty committee most responsible for dealing with student problems, which increasingly were racial ones.

Nobody was adequate to that year of racial strife; the ugliness touched us all. Student groups became strident and revolutionary; certain blacks were Machiavellian in their attempts to exacerbate the racial problems, finding them useful to their ultimate goal of separation. Meanwhile, the faculty split into conservative, liberal, and radical factions, each with a vocal mistrust of the others. Whatever sense of personal virtue I possessed was extinguished by my helplessness to achieve any possible "good" within my faculty committee, composed as it was of a conservative majority that differed, rightly or wrongly, with me on every substantive issue. Often at odds with my own liberal faction, I found myself more than once being false to my own insights (weren't they as dubious as anybody else's?) in order to gain some measure of harmony. If I were a late-twentieth-century character transported into one of T.'s stories—that Jimski who believes in the basic goodness of the human race and who finds a marvelous sense of well-being in communal happenings—, I would at this point reveal my contradictions in a passionate speech to a friend about greed and general human nastiness.

Whatever their inconsistencies, liberals believe in a single societal heart, beating out the same stream of blood to each of us. With the sadness that comes from recognition of their and others' imperfection, they resign themselves, for the sake of the whole organism, to certain discrepanices in the purity and supply of blood to the outlying regions. T. was a liberal by his actions and words, even though he eschewed membership in the club, perhaps waiting for the day on which the heart was, according to his diagnosis, in a healthier state. During that chaotic year at the university, the pattern of slight deceptions I made for the sake of my faction's effectiveness, the small compromises of personal conviction, came to constitute a burden I hadn't realized I was carrying until one day I caught myself in a seemingly trivial act that I immediately felt to be a clear violation of my ideal self. Occasionally a moment comes, in lives like mine, in which the offense against the self is so small that we readily acknowledge it—and, once having done so, are crushed by its symbolic importance as a statement of our nature. In my case, it was simply an incident I came to regard as a demeaning wish to be well regarded by my associates.

Leaving, long before it was over, a large meeting of my liberal-minded colleagues and students, both black and white, as my personal protest of a nearly unanimous vote to condemn the university for institutional racism—in the case at point, I knew my faction had its evidence all wrong, and my attempt to disassociate myself from the group was as quick as any reflex action—I nevertheless stopped in the aisle of the auditorium to smile and whisper a few sympathetic words to a young acquaintance. For the suddenness with which I had left my seat and stumbled around the legs of others in my row had drawn the attention of my acquaintance and others, and I wanted anybody who was watching me to know that I was a friendly guy, anything but a racist, a person who disapproved of nothing and was departing simply to take a piss, or something like that. My self-conscious and hypocritical little display of chumminess horrified me in the act of making it, and led to some dreadful dreams. Perhaps a similar moment came to Augustine following that childhood adventure in which he stole some useless pears because he was in a group that wanted to. Unsympathetic readers of the *Confessions* who find his guilt for this act excessive would have even less understanding of mine. I was at that spiritual breaking point, though, at which such an illumination into myself was terrifying. In self-contempt, disliking mankind, apathetic to any possibilities for social or personal change, I withdrew to the embrace and private concerns of my own small family.

My despair accompanied me to Florence; like many another, I came there for escape and the therapy of creative activity. Can one ever reconcile the inner voice calling for truth with the desire for human mutuality? An answer to such an unlikely question eludes rational argumentation. I decided to revise the unsuccessful draft of a play I had written based on *Sir Gawain and the Green Knight* so that it would provide an imaginative or emotional answer; but whatever the curious amalgam of Christian and pagan elements in that medieval narrative, Gawain's story depends upon a social and religious order too firmly established to serve as a meaningful referent for our less certain century. I considered writing a work of fiction in which the protagonist, who believes he wants both truth and brother-hood, comes to discover his misanthropy, his truth-telling ultimately giving him that cold isolation he unconsciously desires above all else. The prospect of telling such a story brought me no joy. For some weeks I was incapable of any activity other than reading novels of another time or look-ing at pictures and statues of people and beasts long dead. By chance, I picked up a copy of T.'s letters at the British Institute library; and I soon began to read everything I could find about that depression of his which in some ways was comparable with my own, its immediate cause perhaps just as trifling and difficult to explain to another, and about the long journey that was his answer to it.

8

At the urging of the green knight (a huge phantasm conjured up from a normal human being by Morgan le Fay to taunt and test the valor of the knights of Camelot), Gawain agreeably cuts off that apparition's head with a single blow of an axe. Undaunted, the body of the green knight vaults into the jeweled saddle of its great green horse, holding its head by the hair; and it is from the lips of that severed head, blood dripping from the wound, that Gawain hears a reminder of the vow he has just made: if the green knight survives the axe, Gawain in a year and a day must seek him out, to bare his own neck for a similar blow.

Had I been able to write my drama, Morgan le Fay would have become the sorceress of the modern consciousness, and the phantasmagoria she creates—the beautiful castle of Hautdesert with its lovely temptress, as well as the gory head that splats upon the floor at Camelot—would have been the hallucinations engendered by our self-doubt, our unfulfilled desires, and our despair. In the medieval romance, of course, Gawain ultimately dispels his phantoms. Although he must make a solitary horseback journey into regions far removed from the influences of Christ and Camelot, the virtues of religion and of Arthur's Court hold him intact—or nearly so. Being human, he is afraid of dying; and so he engages in a deception—the surreptitious wearing of a girdle of green silk braided with gold that the temptress has promised will protect him, a gift that, at her request and to save her reputation, he denies he possesses. In retribution for that lie, the green knight grazes Gawain's neck with a just-whetted axe blade, but respects him sufficiently to inflict no further injury. After brave but unrecorded adventures on his homeward journey, Gawain reaches Camelot, wearing a scar and the girdle as double tokens of the shame he will carry to his grave. But his immediate confession of his fault nourishes the love and admiration his companions bear for this modest knight who went off to what seemed his inevitable death to keep a vow, thus maintaining the honor of Camelot; and, with much laughter, the other knights decide that they too will always wear girdles of bright green for his sake and their own, his confession as well as his bravery having redounded to the greater honor of them all.

A lovely vessel from the past, that narrative holds universal implications; but in Florence I found it difficult to make it a contemporary one without in some way tarnishing its innocence and charm as well as its truth. Gawain's journey, though, was still on my mind as I read about T.'s, coloring it, I suppose, with that aspect of romance which, indebted to the most primitive or basic of myths, seems part of the memory buried deep in each of us. T. has his phantom—that huge bull's head without eyes: sometimes in the stories it is too amorphous to be observed clearly, but it is always a fearful hallucination, a blind threat to life and meaning. Against it, he wears the armor neither of religion nor of a virtuous political state; he has but himself and that hope he has in us, those who are alive now, and in the descendants of our descendants. Impelled by their phantoms into a sometimes beautiful, sometimes terrifying, natural world, Gawain and T. alike are in pursuit of what each most fears: for Gawain, it is his own death; for T., a place of confinement smelling of death. A vegetation myth, however attenuated, would seem to attach to Gawain's story, and not only because of its motif of greenness. The place of his New Year's Day rendezvous with the green knight is a hollow and grass-covered mound of earth, curiously called a chapel. Holes lead into the cave or burrow; it is as claustrophobic as a grave or dungeon. Before this mound, Gawain faces death, with all the bravery he can muster; in giving himself to it, he is miraculously reborn. T. undergoes a somewhat similar rejuvenation. Is it too far-fetched to imagine T.'s journey, as I did for a time in Florence, as that of a modern man who through genetic memory overleaps the centuries to be nurtured by an ancient faith based on the natural cycles? Yes. T. would have found that interpretation even sillier than the others.

But in Florence, of course, I was searching for some simple faith, however primitive it might be, that would release me from paralysis. Upon our arrival, my family had the choice of two large and equally appealing apartments. One was in an old and beautiful villa on that piazza overlooking the city that Henry James once had for his address. The other apartment was a sixteenth-century villa surrounded by olive trees and vineyards, and with distant views of the mountains; and yet it was a short walk from San Miniato and the Piazzale Michelangelo. This villa was built into a hillside; the apartment, which was on the second floor, opened onto its own private garden of flowers and fig trees. Oh, the tedious listing of opposing attributes, the balancing of this against that, which goes on whenever we are unable to make even a choice between two pleasant

living quarters! This second apartment, while promising
greater seclusion and freedom, was to be approached only
through the confinement of a maze—a narrow and twisting
road bordered by high stone walls. We chose the second
apartment possibly because, unlike the first, it wasn't immediately available; while we waited, we took a trip to
Ljubljana, an industrial city in Yugoslavia, for no greater
reason than that Cris, the older son and hence the one
more affected by the turbulence and idealism of the now-
dying decade, was interested in the practice of self-
management by factory workers in that Communist state.

The external world is always a partial reflection of our
souls; to me, the streets of Ljubljana seemed filled with
sad-eyed or surly young hippies. Their long hair and blue
jeans were the disguises of despair. Our immense hotel
resembled a prison or manufacturing plant, and indeed was
the closest approximation to a factory we encountered.
The desk clerk took our passports and contemptuously
tossed us our keys. The numbering of the rooms made no
discernible sense; carrying our luggage, we wandered from
floor to floor, along one dark corridor after another, passing other little groups of tourists also looking at keys and
door numbers and whispering to each other in strange languages. Mirrors lined the walls of the dining room; the
food was mediocre but expensive. Except for our family
and a stout couple whose rudeness—they stared impas-
sively at us throughout our meal—made them natives, that
large room of mirrors was deserted. Whenever I looked up
from my plate, I saw either the eyes of that pair of secret
agents observing our use of knives and forks, or my own
double image—my face and the back of my skull—
repeated into infinity.

Before boarding the steamer at Yaroslavl, T. saw not
only the mud and the misspelling of the signboards, but
people who looked grotesque, as if they were jackdaws
with oversized heads. After Olga left him, he felt lonely,

remembering her with her hair wet, remembering her as a generous and intelligent presence; but he was glad to have no need for conversation. While eating or drinking on shipboard, he watched the other diners and listened to them boast or talk about food. The towns the ship passed were forlorn gray masses; all towns in his country, he decided, were alike. The trees on the banks were still the brown sticks of winter; the ground, splotched with snow, looked diseased. To his family, he wrote about this segment of his trip, "When a cold wind blows and ruffles up the water, which now after the floods is the color of coffee slops, one feels cold and bored and miserable; the strains of a concertina on the bank sound dejected, figures in tattered sheepskins standing motionless in the barges that meet us look as though they were petrified by some unending grief."

As it had been when he boarded the ship, it was raining when he left it at Perm. Here he took a train for the identical town (though with a different name, Ekaterinburg), where he had promised his mother to look up a male relative, in order to patch up some old family quarrel that he was indifferent to. In Ekaterinburg, the rain turned to sleet and snow; the inhabitants were murderous giants, with jutting brows and eyes that were tiny and full of bird-glitter. The relative, who was editor of a local newspaper, was as huge and threatening as everybody else; he paid T. a brief visit at his hotel, showed no inclination to forget the family hostilities, and declared himself too busy to play guide or host. "Go see our museum and the factories and mines," he said. "Maybe tomorrow we can find time to have tea together." With some malice, T. invited *him* for dinner at the hotel, an offer that was refused.

T. spent two days in Ekaterinburg, with the blinds drawn over his windows; he didn't want to see either that refuse-littered town or the heavy snowflakes falling from the gray, late-April sky. On one occasion he left the hotel to buy a bed sheet, a purchase he'd forgotten to make in

Moscow, but returned empty-handed. He was still coughing up blood, and his hemorrhoids were more painful than
ever. At night, the continual clanging of iron—it seemed to
come from every street corner—kept him awake and irritable. His travels by train would end at the next town of any
size, and so the most difficult portion of his trip lay
ahead—thousands of miles to be traversed on primitive
roads, and with few hotels or restaurants at which one
could linger over a morning glass of tea. He was con-
siderably more than a thousand miles from home, and as
yet had escaped from nothing.

II

A Dark Plain
with
Allegorical Figures

9

Early in May, T. reached Tyumen, a town on the western slopes of the Ural Mountains and the terminus of his railroad journey; before him lay an undifferentiated plain. For the first section of road, he hired an old driver with an odd and lightweight carriage, a chaise made of basketwork and pulled by a pair of horses instead of the more conventional troika; T. sat in the basket, thinking himself like a caged goldfinch. The further he traveled, the more he seemed to be retreating into winter. Snow at first lay in patches, then for a time covered the ground even as thin ice formed on the shallow lakes. During the day, the ruts of the road were channels of water, the hooves of the horses came out of the mud with sucking sounds, and the world, so far as one could see, was one vast slough. As night approached, the ruts and clumps of mud froze, permitting a greater speed; but how T. bounced in his cage! What was there for him to see or hear? Thousands upon thousands of

ducks, the air heavy with their fluttering, some of them
swooping down as if to look at that big bird in his cage; the
calling of geese that, like T. himself, perversely were
fleeing spring with its balmy days and budding roses and
blossoming cherry trees; hares at the edge of the road,
bravely standing on their hind legs to watch the lumbering
passage of the four-wheeled phenomenon; snipe and
woodcock in the bare copses—in short, birds and animals
in abundance, but only an occasional human. Such men as
he saw were derelicts, beggars exiled for their crimes—the
sort of people who maim each other in drunken brawls and
kill old peasant women for their ragged clothes, but look
innocently at travelers, with half-kneeling and palms-up
obeisance. Perhaps they felt that even to dream of stealing a
pair of warm socks from an exalted personage in a high and
willowy basket pulled by well-fed horses would result in
fierce floggings by the invisible authorities. And as T.
traveled on, the monotonous landscape seemed ever more
empty, an emptiness somehow intensified at night by the
snakes of flame in the distance, fires set to burn the fields
before the ploughing: a token that people, however unob-
served, still existed, and believed a new season to be approaching.

    How does one try to understand what it felt like to be
T. at this point of his adventure? His schedule and perhaps
the condition of the post stations—his latest biographer
refers to them as notorious for their inhospitality and
bugs—kept him from putting up for the night. Waiting at a
post station for fresh horses and his next driver, T. would
fall instantly asleep in a chair or against the wall, to be
awakened by a huge, bearded face that was part of some
larger dream—"Time to go, mate!"—in half an hour. He
wrote that he was too numb—he meant this in both a
physical and spiritual sense—to feel or think, though this
wasn't quite true. His hemorrhoids were painful and his
feet, cramped in new boots, hurt so much that he worried
about frostbite; and his memory was working, making

comparisons of this plain with the southern one he had frequently visited as a child living in the town by the sea.

In trying to find feelings in my past commensurate with what his must have been, I can only recall moments in which an inner desolation was defined by an opposing sensation. On an August night in 1943, beneath a Georgia moon, my infantry basic training battalion—while on a forced march up and down hills, through pine woods and cornfields, across the stones of dry creek beds, and along country roads—crossed a railroad track, perhaps a spur line to nothing more than a cotton gin. Basic training gave me my only extended experience as a buffoon or pariah: a pacifist by nature and schooling caught up in a necessary war, I hated guns so much that I fell asleep on the day each member of my platoon had to put together the disassembled parts of a Browning automatic rifle with eyes closed; I became physically ill after I was issued a bayonet for the M-1 rifle that was part of my personal equipment; I was so poor an infantryman, so resentful of the daily attempts to obliterate my separate identity, that I was twice threatened with the stockade; and, as a punishment strictly in accordance with military logic, I was the only member of my special platoon (the rest were sent to college to learn foreign languages and calculus) to be shipped out to a division being readied for combat in France. In any event, crossing that railroad track, I purposely broke step so that my boot would touch the rail: full of hopeless longing, unhappier than I'd ever been, I knew that the track—those two rails curving off, blue and glittering, into obscurity—connected with other tracks that led to every city in America, including Cleveland, where Jean, the girl I wanted to marry, lay sleeping in a little house a few blocks from the East Seventy-first Street station. To touch the rail was such a blessing that my despondency was rich and meaningful, a necessary condition for an instant of grace which made eternal a bit of the world. The corner sections of a fence, just beyond the crossing, were and are of wood,

painted white, and have diagonals to support the end post;
a cow stands near the corner, and the night breeze, unexpectedly cool, brings the scent of freshly-mown hay. A
hundred yards beyond the crossing we come to a dark
hamlet, where the battalion turns right at an intersection
by a store with a Dr. Pepper sign, heading down a dirt road
into a darkness that a now-fading memory will never illuminate.

Any conscious attempt to remember despair is to remember the happiness of hope; despair itself is but its absence. T.'s lifelong hopefulness was nourished now only
by his goal—a prison colony inhabited (as best as he could
imagine) by suffering human shades. For T. there were no
railroad tracks, only the mud of a plain whose other chief
characteristic—its unending flatness—was, like all else in
his world, infected with illusion: the gentle curve of the
horizon, perceived in the flush of a false dawn, declared
that what was flat was also quite round, and curved back
upon itself. He had only his memory of childhood trips
across another plain—not a muddy one like this, though it
too had birds and animals. On that other plain was something in the distance, a tower which might be a windmill,
that stayed visible for hours, its position altering as the
road imperceptibly curved; and at night there was the
glow, like a phosphorescent rose, of distant lightning behind heavy clouds. There were small swellings on the
earth—ancient tumuli—, and crosses marking the graves of
merchants who had been set upon by brigands.

In the long story that won for T. his first acclaim as a
serious writer, he had written of a young boy,
Egorooshka, who journeys for days across that plain,
traveling on one of the wagons of a caravan taking bales of
wool to market. One night Egorooshka sits in a circle of
lonely and dissatisfied peasants around a small fire beneath
the indifferent stars; the flames illuminate two burial
crosses, and a peasant, inspired by them as well as by the
darkness beyond the fire, tells a series of stories, each of

which invokes terror dispelled by a supernatural interven-
tion that stays the sharp knife approaching the victim's
throat. Suddenly a stranger—a hunter bearing a large
bird—appears. He is young and recently married, a man so
full of happiness that he must seek out people, however
dispersed in this vastness they are, to tell them of his great
good fortune in love, of the rapture that gives him his
exquisite pain on this night that his bride has gone off to
see her mother; his smiles are as mysterious to the peasants
as any tale about a merchant with a knife at his throat. Had
T. himself, as a boy, observed such a happy man on that
plain? And had there actually been peasants who were first
dissatisfied and then so awed by what to them was an
apparition of pure happiness coming out of the dark that
one of them afterwards sang a sacred song and another
raised a senseless cry about the greatness of their mother
country? Half-asleep in the jolting chaise, T. remembered
a stranger who perhaps never had existed except in his own
imagination, and felt the wonder and strangeness of his
smile, as if he were one of those discontented and simple
peasants. Lost as they may be in a slough too extensive for
comprehension, travelers like T. carry as part of their mental baggage their life work; and sometimes it can be as
serviceable as a leather coat or a cylinder of salami.

But then he slept, and saw his brother Nicholas in the
coffin; salami, leather coats, and imaginary happy strangers alike became useless before that corpse and the
meaninglessness even of grief. "Smarter than I!" he cried in
his sleep, and immediately saw that huge and eyeless bull's
head; it was sporadically visible, like a black cloud in a
thunderstorm. He woke with a sour taste in his mouth,
and spat blood over the side of the chaise. "You have but
one failing, dear brother," he said to the dead Nicholas,
remembering his own words of advice—they had repre-
sented his belief that he might yet save his brother from
alcoholism and consumption, if Nicholas would but emu-
late *his* moderation and general way of life: "You lack

culture." Those words, so foolish and unctuous, made him
wish to swill vodka. Although it was snowing again, he felt
feverish; and he wondered if he had come to this dark
emptiness because it was such a suitable environment for
death.

If. T.'s journey was indeed a quest for rebirth, the old
self—that numb but still suffering consciousness or ego,
that dark and moist breeding ground of his hallucinations—had to die, as surely as the snake scales which wind
and weather had made of his facial skin would eventually
have to be cast off; and one morning, just before dawn, an
event occurred that permitted this to happen. The wet
snow and rains had held off for several days. His driver
was an elderly man who seemed (was it just T.'s mood,
more passive than usual?) free of the sullen brutality he had
come to expect. Even T.'s memory was quiescent; the
aroma of the ever-present burning fields and birch copses
gave him no images from his childhood or youth and spoke
to him neither of spring nor autumn. Suddenly three heavy
troikas, all mail carts, came looming out of the grayness
ahead, one after the other. The driver of the first was lashing his horses, apparently to make up for lost time, but the
drivers of the following were asleep, their horses galloping
simply to keep up with the preceding one. The first troika
veered around T.'s much smaller trap, but the second col-
lided directly with it; the horses of both vehicles reared and
fell, thrashing to free themselves from the harnesses and
neighing in terror. T. was catapulted out of his trap as it
overturned, his luggage landing on top of him. He rolled
off the road and scrambled to his feet, screaming "Stop!
Stop!" to the third driver, who, waking, managed to slow
his horses enough so that, although they became entangled
in the wreckage, the cart was not damaged.

Afterwards, in a letter to Mary and the other family
members, T. tried to capture the atmosphere of the crash

and of what followed; his driver—that "very nice old man"—and the other drivers

> fell to abusing each other ferociously. Oh, how they swore! I thought it would end in a fight. You can't imagine the feeling of isolation in the middle of that savage swearing crew in the open country, just before dawn, in sight of the fires far and near consuming the grass, but not warming the cold night air! Oh, how heavy my heart was! One listened to the swearing, looked at the broken shafts and at one's tormented luggage, and it seemed as though one were cast away in another world, as though one would be crushed in a moment.

But elsewhere this letter—to my knowledge, the longest one that T. wrote on this trip—is full of an extraordinary exuberance. Written ten days after the accident, it comments on the pleasure of tea for a traveler and on T.'s liking for the peasant food of the region, particularly for the delicious fish soup and splendid white bread. It notes that smallpox is strangely less contagious here than elsewhere despite the primitive medical practices, and that diphtheria is nonexistent. His own health has miraculously improved: not only is his appetite voracious, but his cough with its bloody sputum is gone, his hemmorrhoids are no longer swollen and painful, he has not even the slightest of headaches; and, as is apparent from his other correspondence, whenever he is granted the boon of a bed with a feather mattress in the immaculate cottage of a peasant, he enjoys sleep immensely. The letter reveals a renewal of his curiosity about, and admiration for, people: the plain, recently so empty, now is populated with a kindly and intelligent folk. It is as if T. is a Gulliver who has left the Yahoos in their identical filthy towns for a stay in the country with the noble, but wholly human, Houyhnhnms.

The peasant women are free of male domination, being the physical and mental equals of their husbands, and both men and women are as tender-hearted as they are industrious and capable. Parents love their children, allowing them to sleep in the morning as late as they wish; if a father laughs at his son or daughter, the child will scold him for his condescension, however affectionate the laughter may have been. What a difference from T.'s own upbringing! In this land, children, like women, like Jews and other minority groups, are accorded a dignity that prevents their treatment as lesser creatures. As for the Jews, they work as drivers, farmers, ferrymen; universally respected, they frequently are chosen as village elders. Exiled Poles marry natives, and breed black-eyed and soft-featured boys and girls. T.'s entire country is blessed: "My God," he exclaims, "how rich we are in good people!"

It won't do to impose any of our century's reductive labels upon T.'s soul, to see his elation and returning health as the manic phase of a manic-depressive personality. Like all of us, he had his ups and downs; but—except for that extended period that ended with the wreck and the terrifying vision of aloneness in that alien underworld of cold flames, thrashing animals, and cursing human brutes—he had always been the one that others counted upon for stability, humor, and practical advice. The rational contentment he saw everywhere about him a week or so after his accident was, as he recognized, at least partly the consequence of economic conditions—these particular peasants owned generous portions of fertile farmland—but he was suddenly open to it as the brave new world of his returned idealism. The episode with the three mail carts was strange enough to seem, in retrospect, a medieval allegory with a cast of demons, the sort of adventure that belongs in a fictional work like *Don Quixote*. As an example of randomness in life, it was nothing he could have willed. And yet it or some other rehearsal of his death was, I think, an unconscious part of his purpose in undertaking his expedition, much as it must have been part of an infirm Cervantes' in sending his knight out on the last journey.

It is not so odd as it first might appear that one most fears death during those intervals in which life most approximates it, and seems pointless. And if one values freedom above all else, it may seem to lie—especially as it constricts into an ever more hopeless and solipsistic yearning—within the death that is so intensely feared: caught in a spiritual paralysis, one exists in a sort of death-in-life. While still in Moscow, T. was sufficiently aware of that danger to know that he had to move, even if it were but a physical movement across a continent to an arbitrarily-chosen goal. What he really needed to know, though, was that his desire for freedom was not a death wish, however much it had drawn him toward the solitude of sky and plain and the grandeur of mountains that, still lying ahead, were but a dream to him of banks of evergreens fragrant with resin in the splendid sunlight, forests rising silently toward bare rock and lonely snow-covered summits gleaming in their rarefied and intoxicating air; he needed to know that (however much one wants a unity to which consciousness itself is the final barrier) freedom and death are contradictory terms.

His brush with the frigid isolation and mean constriction of death rescued him from his fearful attraction toward it, and returned him to life. How else does one explain his renewed interest and belief in people and the reckless self-confidence and exultation he felt on the day immediately following the accident?

10

On the morning after the accident, the wind picked up, driving sheets of rain horizontally across the plain; toward evening, T. arrived, quite soaked despite the canopy over his cart, at the last post house before the Irtysh River. He had bought felt boots to replace his tight-fitting jackboots; intended for snow, they already had become limp and useless as wet cardboard. His driver, who lived in the hamlet, led the horses, their heads lowered in weariness and their necks and backs steaming in the downpour, toward the stable behind the station for grain and hay and a grooming: "More care than I'll get at home, or you'll get in there," he said cheerfully, pointing toward the post house, a cottage made of stones. In the building, three waiting drivers—two old men and a young one—were languidly playing cards with a tattered and greasy deck; the innkeeper sat nearby, drinking vodka and scratching first one armpit and then the other. A mixture of mud and manure in the shape of boot prints was caked on the plank floor. Hens clucked in the adjoining room; one had escaped from her cage, and eyed T. from the doorway. The room was warm, for the stove was burning, and smelled of damp wood smoke, bodies, acrid bird droppings, and something more pleasant—the fragrance of grain in the bags stacked against one wall.

"Tea, vodka, an egg?" the innkeeper asked, intoning his entire menu without bothering to rise; for T., with his scaly face, unkempt beard, and cheap boots that squished at every step, appeared to be but another peasant forced by some sorry emergency—a death or illness nobody wanted to hear about—to squander his money on a journey for a relative or a priest. But then the innkeeper saw that T.'s coat was, despite its muddy smears, an expensive leather one, tailored to fit his body, and he rose to his feet, bowing. "I have a bottle of the good sort hidden away," he said. "Certainly, sir, a glass of it and a comfortable bed for the night! If the rain eases up tomorrow and the wind stops its howling, perhaps the water will drain off the fields: they say it comes in waves, a gentleman would be drowned. Now, let us take your boots and dry them on the stove," and he reached down to remove them.

"No," T. said, putting one boot down so firmly that the water under his heel squeaked like a mouse. One of the tendencies he had always disliked in himself was his readiness to agree with another, simply to be polite, to avoid offense; ever since taking to the roads he had allowed himself to be lied to by mercenary innkeepers and to accept inferior carriages at twice the going rate. He could tell at once from the mock obsequiousness ("Surely such an intelligent and well-bred personage as yourself would want . . .") that he was being cheated; but he disliked haggling, especially with anybody less fortunate than he was. That morning, though, he had struck a fair bargain with his driver, and been respected for it. He felt more

resolute than he had in months. And so he turned to the
card players to ask, "Who's going to drive me?"

The youngest, a muscular peasant barely more than a
boy, and one of the older, a small and wizened man with a
goiter, looked at the third, a man whose coat was spotted
and ripped at the seams but whose great white beard and
erect bearing gave him the appearance of an old general
unfairly deprived of his pension. He cleared his throat, as if
he were a person of importance about to express a considered opinion. "It's my rightful turn, and once I would
have been glad enough to take it. When I was younger, I
was known throughout the countryside as the best driver
in the world. I was the one that taught these two their
trade, even George here," and he nodded at the other old
man. "Would you guess he's six years my junior? I look
healthier, and would be except for my spells—it's my
heart, when I get too wrought up. And so now I'm known
for my sharpness with cards. It's a bore to play cards in
foul weather, to win hand after hand from two people who
always are forgetting the rules; but God determines what
we can do today as well as what we did yesterday. Do you
play cards, sir?"

"Not when I'm in a hurry," T. said.

"Perhaps, if you stay the night, we could have a foursome. Yuri—" and now he nodded at the innkeeper—"is
too lazy for cards. We drivers play not for money, but for
straws, and that makes all men equal. You see, sir, they say
the river's so far beyond its banks you can't find the road—
though I could, if my heart would let me: I could get to the
ferry with my eyes closed!—and some of the bridges
gone."

"Who says that, grandfather?" T. asked.

"Kuzma."

"I was the one that talked with Kuzma," the young
driver said. "But Igor speaks the truth. Kuzma says it may
be three or four days before anybody reaches the ferry. He

got only halfway there, and had a hard time finding enough solid ground to turn his horses."

"And what if you somehow got to the ferry, what then?" George, the one with the goiter, asked. More timid than the others, he spoke in a rush, his voice excited and high-pitched. "The ferrymen are a hard sort, exiled for their crimes, but, as Kuzma says, they won't risk their necks for a traveler, if the current's strong and the wind too high. That's really why Kuzma turned back," and he looked at his companions triumphantly, as if his were the telling remark.

"Where is this Kuzma?" T. asked, leaning against one of the grain bags and staring at the innkeeper, who had returned to his chair and once again was complacently scratching an armpit. For these drivers, even the young one, were speaking only from hearsay, and it was possible that Kuzma had been bribed by the innkeeper to keep a traveler like him stranded in this hole for three or four days, an eternity.

Yuri laughed. "You won't find Kuzma now, that's for sure," he said. He turned to face the young peasant who had talked with Kuzma. "Peter, you tell him where Kuzma might be, in all this rain."

The young man blushed. "With his bride," he said in a low voice, almost a whisper, looking at the floor.

It was obvious to T. that Peter was still unmarried, but probably had a girl in one of the neighboring villages, and was lonely for her. T. himself felt a far greater loneliness than he had yet experienced on this trip, even when saying goodbye to his family and to Olga: the feeling was so strong and abrupt that it shocked him, and with it came an anxiety for his mother, an old woman who might fall again while he was away. His loneliness was bound to that strange new exaltation which the storm outside—a shutter banged, the rain beat at the window—only intensified. The warmth, the dusty fragrance of the grain, opened his mem-

ory to sensations from his childhood, from a period long
before his father's business failed, and he remembered a
vacation on his grandfather's farm (it was on that other
plain) and particularly the pleasure, including stops for
picnics and swimming, of the slow trip toward the farm.
He remembered, too, smelling the grass blades (next to his
eye, they were huge in the evening dark, like tropical
plants) as he lay on his stomach in the garden of his childhood home: for on hot nights the children were permitted
to sleep outside. From the house came the deliberate chime
of the clock, the sound of his father's violin and his
mother's voice, gentle and young, in accompaniment.
When he turned to lie on his back, he could see, through
the still leaves of the grape arbor that sheltered him like a
cave, the movement of a planet as it drifted behind a leaf.
His two older brothers talked and laughed in a distant
corner of the garden, and some other child, jealous perhaps
of their comradeship, called for them to hush; when eventually they did, but only after the house windows had
darkened, there came the insistent surge of summer insects
to fill the silence.

   It seemed to T. that the present, this crowded and
dirty room, opened both backwards and forwards into different but equally intriguing landscapes, and that desire
itself, which went both ways, was rich and meaningful. He
had insight not only into Peter but into all the others
caught in this wretched post house, including the innkeeper Yuri, content as he was to scratch himself and to
drink vodka while exploiting anybody who came his
way—after all, T. had observed and written of people like
these many times over. How much, for example, did
George's swollen thyroid gland, that disfigurement he was
always touching, contribute to his timidity and bursts of
talk? But it was so ludicrous to imagine himself confined
with them—playing cards for days on end with boastful
old Igor—that he laughed; and Igor, thinking that T., like
the innkeeper, was laughing at the alacrity with which

Kuzma, who had tried but failed to master the elements, had hopped into bed with his bride, said, with some contempt for Kuzma, "Getting married is like getting drunk—it makes some men daring and others fearful," and began an account of how, as a recently-married man, he had forced his horses into a stream so swift and deep that the floating cart pulled the horses a quarter-mile downstream, and not even a single harness strap had become entangled.

How simple it was for T. to get his way! Shamelessly, he displayed such admiration for Igor's youthful exploits that the old driver became ever more expansive. It was difficult to tell how much Igor exaggerated or lied; George nodded at every detail as if it were common knowledge, and added a few more modest adventures of his own. Peter, meanwhile, grew defensive and restless, and T. waited for the proper moment to say that he would trust Peter as a driver, if Igor thought the trip could be made. Although it meant the loss of his foursome, Igor now encouraged Peter to go, for this storm was a blustery trifle to any youth of spirit. When Peter shrugged and left the building to harness his horses, Yuri shouted angrily after him, "You'll see, you'll come back just like Kuzma," but by the time T. was struggling to get his luggage through the door, Yuri had lost interest in both of them and was yawning and scratching and pouring himself more vodka.

The wind had increased, making it impossible for T. to speak to Peter; and the rain, as it hit his face, stung. But for the first half hour or so the road was the same morass he had been accustomed to for much of the journey across the plain. The spokes of the cart wheels came up dripping with water and mud from the twin ruts that had become narrow streams, and it seemed as if the wheels were paddles effortlessly propelling the cart onward, for the sound of the horses and of Peter's cries to them was lost in the whistling of the wind. Finally, T. could see the river in the distance, or at least the far bank of it, which, despite the rain, was ghostly with snow. The road, instead of proceed-

ing directly to the river, turned to run parallel with it, the
ferry crossing being some miles upstream. Now the fields
were flooded and the road ahead a narrow causeway across
a lake that went onward as far as one could see. The cart
stopped. Was it here that Kuzma had decided to go back?
Peter looked back at T., shouting something; T. waved
him on, for that sense of lonely exaltation remained with
him as a stubborn determination, and it was inconceivable
that they would return to the little room where Yuri
waited, a complacent spider. The cart wheels began revolv-
ing again; they were on the causeway—actually, a spine of
mud that on occasion dipped beneath the water—and it
was too late to turn back.

Once T. had taken his family for an excursion aboard
a yacht on the Black Sea. Perhaps he had recently re-
covered from an illness, and felt the exhilaration that accompanies the return to good health; at any rate, on
impulse, as the yacht slowly drifted, he jumped from the
deck for a swim, terrifying Mary. The abandonment in
falling first through the air and then deeply into a liquid
darkness—that great bowl with a shimmering, blue-gold
cover—increased his pleasure in being alive, and made his
body feel sensual and strong; and that same kind of stubborn ardor was with him now. In his long letter to Mary
and the others, he compared that dive from the ship with
his decision to continue onward, seeing both as examples
of his "incomprehensible impulse of defiance"—although
here there was no warm sunshine and tranquil blue sea, but
cold rain splattering down on brown water and nothing
else to see in the somber light but that long and mysterious
bank of snow which told of a river yet to be crossed. No
bridges spanning the smaller streams had been washed
away, but their approaches had been; salvaged planks
served as temporary approaches, and two of the three
horses had to be unhitched before each bridge and led
separately across the planks. T. held the unharnessed
horses, the water as deep in his limp boots as it was outside

them. Peter was anything but a spirited youth as he unbuckled and then buckled each harness strap; water dripping from his cap into his eyes, his clothing soaked, he was abject, and T., the cause of his misery, felt sorry for him, and determined to add handsomely to the fare they had agreed upon, regardless of his earlier resolution to make and hold to a bargain.

Night had fallen by the time a mound of earth, almost an island, loomed ahead. Horses wandered across this dome of thickets, hungry refugees from the flooded pastures; the ground was pocked with hoof prints and manure. On this mound, the road, such as it was, seemed to end. In a scene that to T. was as heightened as the allegory of the previous day, a peasant came out of a roofless hut bearing a long stick and motioned for them to follow him. He splashed through the water, testing its depth and the firmness of the submerged ground, leading the cart into the lake until they reached a bit of land; here the peasant pointed his stick across the water in the direction of the next ridge. To T., he was an augury of good fortune, a guide who, in blessing them, was himself blessed; and from the cart moving across the water, T. watched as the peasant—standing like a small statue on the hillock, wand in hand—vanished behind them in the rain and darkness.

Soon thereafter, they reached the ferry crossing. The Irtysh, one of the major rivers draining the plain, frothed into white waves near the eroded clay bank which rose barely a yard above the current; farther out in the muddy water, ice floes glided swiftly by. The ferry, a long and wide-bottomed barge with oarlocks, was lashed by thick ropes to posts. The landscape was devoid of trees or any other vegetation; behind them lay the lake they had crossed, before them the river, oddly silent in its fierce movement except for a continual booming, muffled as if— this was the analogy that came to T. that night, waiting for sleep in a tiny room of the ferrymen's hut, for they indeed refused to carry him across until the wind abated the fol-

lowing day—someone were pounding on a coffin beneath
the surface, a hammering sound that belonged with the
cold fires and blaspheming demons of the immediate past.

T.'s journey to Sakhalin made its effect on a number
of his stories, but two in particular were a consequence of
specific experiences. The first story, completed while he
was still aboard the steamer on his homeward voyage, was
based on events, including a burial at sea, that he observed
as a passenger on the ship. The other, written several years
later, may be a lesser achievement—I measure all of T.'s
literary work, and that of many other writers I admire,
against that first story—but it is a companion to it nevertheless. This second story is about exile, and the seeming
opposition of desire and freedom; its source is the night he
spent in the ferrymen's hut as the wind continued to gust,
the rain to beat against the roof, the river to boom, while
the ferrymen—those rough exiles—snored with his driver
in the adjoining room.

The two major characters are a toothless old ferryman, Semyon—alas, a year younger than I am!—and
another exile, an unnamed Tatar of twenty-five who for a
pittance wields one of the oars of the ferry during the
spring floods. The young Tatar tells old Semyon that he
has been unfairly accused of stealing a horse and beating its
owner. He longs for his freedom and his native province;
he longs for his wife, who may come with his mother to
live with him in exile after his father, who is ill, dies; but he
knows the impossibility of this wished-for happiness, for
he has no real livelihood—like many other exiles, he wanders about the plain most of the year, begging for food and
clothes. Unlike the Tatar's, Semyon's previous life has
been one of comfort; the son of a deacon, he lived as a
youth in a provincial city, where he was accustomed to
freedom and fashionable clothes. But upon his exile he
renounced desire so completely that (or so he says) he
yearns for nothing, neither love of a woman nor any mate-

rial possession; for twenty-two years he has been content to ferry passengers back and forth across the river, he on top of the water and the pike and salmon beneath it. His home is the ferrymen's hut; weather permitting, he would gladly sleep naked on the ground and eat grass. To the Tatar, filled with a desire so hopeless he is wasting away— he is sick, shivering—, the old ferryman is cruel and life-denying. One must always aspire to happiness, however transitory it may be. God, who created man to live and to know both joy and sorrow, cannot possibly love a beast without wants. To Semyon—who, despite his age, is ro-bust—desire is evil, the work of the devil. True freedom comes only to one capable of renouncing desire absolutely.

To prove the superiority of his position, Semyon tells the Tatar of a well-to-do gentleman, a member of the no-bility, who, exiled to this region fifteen years previously for forgery, decided he could become happy here, and so entered upon a new life as a farmer; he convinced his beau-tiful young wife to join him, bringing their infant daugh-ter. Crossing the ferry with his newly-arrived family on their way to their new home, the gentleman in his joy called out, "Yes, brother Semyon, even in Siberia people can live!" After three years of living among people devoid of culture, the depressed wife slipped away with a young official, leaving the child behind; the gentleman galloped fruitlessly here and there in pursuit first of her and then of his freedom—in person, he petitioned one regional bureau-crat after another, and he wrote countless letters to officials in the west. As the daughter grew, though, he transferred his affection to her; she became the central meaning of his life. But as she matured into an attractive and lively young person, she, like her mother, came to feel her situation intolerable, and in her discontent fell victim to consump-tion. At the present time the girl is so ill, Semyon remarks, that her father is continually galloping about the country-side in search of a new doctor with some miraculous cure; but her death is certain, and when it occurs, the gentleman will either take his own life or try to escape. If he chooses the latter course, he inevitably will be caught, whipped, and sentenced to hard labor.

Were the two major antagonists of this story based on actual ferrymen whom T. met that stormy night he spent in the hut on the banks of the Irtysh? Probably not. Before falling asleep, he wrote a brief letter to an old friend, Mary Kiselyov, who with her husband owned an estate at Bab-kino, where T. and his family and their guests had enjoyed a particularly happy summer five years earlier. The ferry-men, he writes her, are good-natured people; after all, they could have robbed him and drowned him in the river. In the long letter to his sister and family, he says that the ferrymen are rowdy, use bad language, and ask for money to buy vodka; but he mentions nobody with the frightening austerity of Semyon. It is likely that Semyon and the young Tatar are composites of people he encoun-tered—not only exiles but innkeepers and drivers like the ones I have called Yuri and Peter as well as a serene old convict who transported people across a river in a box-like little ferry at the prison colony; beyond that, of course, they are aspects of his own nature.

T.'s Semyon, though disciplined in his nonattach-ment, is far from saintly. His withdrawal is imperfect in its motives, revealing a self-centeredness at its base. He is not only spiteful but greedy for the one commodity he still values. As the story opens, we are told that Semyon is putting off going to his bed in the hut because he has a bottle of vodka in his pocket that he wants to drink with-out sharing it with the others. His spite is directed against those who, like the Tatar and the gentleman, continue to affirm life through hope and grief. As the story nears its end, the gentleman calls in a fury from the opposite shore for the barge; his daughter's condition has worsened, and he has heard of yet another new doctor. In his role as narrator, T. comments that the four ferrymen plying their oars in the darkness—Semyon, the fifth, is at the tiller—

seem like men "sitting on some antediluvian animal with long paws, and sailing to a cold, bleak land, the very one of which we sometimes dream in nightmares." The barge has become Charon's; after picking up the gentleman—he has become thin and elderly in exile—, Semyon, that steersman and spokesman for death, taunts his passenger about his long-ago expression of joy, "Even in Siberia people can live," repeating that last word with a drawling and bitter emphasis.

In the final scene, Semyon, having consumed all of the vodka, goes into the hut to lie down with the other ferrymen; outside, meanwhile, the young Tatar howls his grief like a dog. The implication is that one drawn to life and its affirmations can be reduced, through brutality and injustice and unfulfilled desires, to a level as animalistic as that of a Semyon who would deny human love and all hope. T.'s own voice is carried in that howl; responding to it, one feels a compassion for the Tatar that extends to provide, if not sympathy for, at least an understanding of Semyon and the suffering he would avoid.

This story is one of the first that T. wrote as the proprietor of that country estate he had dreamed of for many years—at least since that happy summer with the Kiselyovs. In remembering for the sake of the story his night in the hut on the bank of the swollen Irtysh, did he also recall the note he wrote, in exhaustion and under dim lamplight, that same night to Mary Kiselyov, the dismal view of the water and the barge and the muffled booming of the river having brought to his mind a mysterious pool which once apparently terrified that gay and imprudent woman? The desolation that T. found at the river was wholly in keeping with his depression before the three mail carts crashed into his trap, but now it reminded him of his affection and sympathy for an old friend, and perhaps of the terror of death that her abandon had concealed. T.'s literary work usually avoids the allegorical quality that is present in the story he wrote from his experiences and sensations at the ferrymen's hut; that quality, though, is in keeping with his responses to actual events during this period of his journey. He himself had thrown off death for life, and wanted to get on to his goal, which must have gained in meaning.

The next morning, the weather improved enough for the ferrymen to row him to the opposite shore. The booming sound he now heard was of a different sort—it was the thumping call of the male bitterns, those birds of the heron family that he had seen and listened to in summertime on several estates in the more southerly parts of Russia; their appearance here surprised and gratified T. He clambered up the slippery clay and snow on the other side of the river, and traveled on through the rain to find his happy families and to enjoy their white bread and fish soup and their clean beds. Exultation, that extraordinary sense of well-being in the service of life, releases a person from himself, and hence is as harmonious to the soul as it is to the body; but exultation cannot last, and its ebbing can leave one exposed to all the horrors that humans inflict upon themselves and each other.

11

Our life in Florence soon settled into a routine that would have been exceedingly pleasant for me had I been capable of accomplishing anything I considered worthwhile. Each morning Jean and our two sons left for school. Jean drove Jimmy to his, and then headed down the hill and across the Arno to the University of Florence for lessons in Italian; Cris preferred to walk down the steps behind the Piazzale Michelangelo to reach his classes—in Italian and Renaissance culture—at the British Institute. I sat at a desk by the opened window in Jean's and my bedroom, looking at a blank sheet of paper or at the view of olive groves, neighboring earthen-colored old villas, and mountains in the distance. Sometimes I met Jean for luncheon at a tiny restaurant in an alley near Dante's presumed house; whether we ate together or not, we would spend the afternoons—until it was time to pick up Jimmy—in the galleries, churches, palaces, markets, and

public gardens. Without a television set, Jimmy became as
engrossed in books as Jean and I had been as children; as
she was preparing dinner, he sat at the marble-topped
kitchen table, reading aloud from novels borrowed from
the school library. Cris had a late class, and we waited for
dinner until he returned in the dark: "I'm home," he would
call cheerfully from the vestibule, and Jean would light the
candle on the dining-room table by the French doors overlooking our garden.

On weekends we visited those surrounding cities and
towns whose names still give me a pleasure to pronounce,
one after the other—Bologna, Modena, Lucca, Pisa, Siena,
San Gimignano, Volterra, Montepulciano (where we
bought our wine, having our demijohn filled, for the
equivalent of about thirty cents a liter, with *vino nobile*
from one of the huge wooden casks in a cool and fragrant
cave that had been a winery since the ninth century), Per-
ugia, Assisi, Gubbio; each possessed such a culture, was
such a world in itself, that this geographical circle with
Florence at the center seemed larger than the entire United
States.

Of the smaller hill towns, I was especially drawn to
Volterra. Driving up the winding road to it, one sees first a
sprawling fortress with towers and ramparts—severe and
forbidding, it is used as a prison. Perhaps the prison has
come to symbolize the town, preventing it from becoming
a tourist attraction in the manner of the neighboring San
Gimignano with its forest of improbable towers; but Volterra affords a more romantic panorama of rugged mountains and more dramatic sunsets, the grandeur of its vistas
suggesting a freedom beyond confinement. The fortress
and the huge stone blocks of its Etruscan gate impart to
Volterra itself a sense of permanence. At the opposite side
of the town, though, the hillside is eroding away; former
landslides are frozen into chaotic masses in the valley and a
church perches precariously near the edge. The majority of
the people live and work between the fortress and the erod-

ing slope; many of them are artisans, using the prevalent alabaster to make polished and often imaginative artifacts, which they sell in the shop of their workers' cooperative. Every time we visited Volterra, we had coffee and Cokes at a small café whose owner would instruct us in the subtleties of his language—the many names for our word "table," for instance—and would call his dog Ringo to entertain us by walking on his hind legs. I knew of two writers who had visited Volterra. Perhaps affected too much by the grimness of its prison and some of its *palazzi,* D. H. Lawrence found it the most depressing of his Etruscan places. Stendhal, passionately in love with the idea of love—that is, with a beautiful Parisian actress who spurned his advances—, pursued her to Volterra, wearing for disguise a trench coat, dark glasses, and a false nose; but she recognized the man following her through the streets of that little town, and became so angry that he panicked and fled.

Being in love with the idea of love—Augustine's *amabam amare*—is itself a disguise for, or a displacement of, spiritual longing; it is a desire for what exists on Earth only as hope or promise, and feeds on its own awareness of separation and loss. In a place even more remote and austere than Volterra—the monastery at Camaldoli, tucked in a pine-forested high valley near the Apennine crest—I was once surprised, even shocked, by what I thought to be the appeal that monastic life held for me. But that appeal really was for my projected lonely love, in separation from my wife and children, in my life with my fellow monks, and simply proved that I was closer in spirit to Stendhal than to Lawrence. The attraction that Volterra held for me seemed a different matter, for I saw it as a hilltop island on which men and women embraced and fought and mated, and brotherhood took on a political meaning—the workers' cooperative, part of an attempt at a communism devoid of tyranny, flourished, despite the looming presence of the prison—as well as a spiritual one. I dreamed of an improbable stay at Volterra—say, during my next sabbatical leave—in which my wife and children and I, our ages and attitudes unchanged, would live for a year with the café owner and his dog Ringo and the alabaster workers, some of whom we had met in a restaurant, and from them would learn subtleties about more than just the Italian language. But of course I knew so little about them that now I remember only the name of the dog. I was imparting to them the qualities of my own desire for a spiritual and physical fusion; this also was a love of the idea of love, and I was nearly fifty and much too old for such adolescent yearning.

As I sat at my desk during our first months in Florence, an image from my actual adolescence came to me each morning: the image of dark ground, a pasture or hay field overgrown with brush and illuminated by the full moon. It was a memory, really, of an early compulsion to write that I had felt after my father had lost our house and deserted his family. Without resources, my mother and brother and I had moved in with relatives, and I felt humiliated and unwanted, whatever the hospitality of my uncle and aunt. One summer evening a boyfriend of one of my cousins—a girl, older than I—came to take her for a ride in his Model A Ford roadster and, with a generosity difficult for me to believe, invited my brother and me to come along in the rumble seat, open to the warm night air. He parked by the edge of a field to view the moonlit landscape. It was a still night. I could hear crickets and frogs and the cry of a bird; at the end of the field there lay a snaking trail of mist, probably above an unseen creek. What I wished for were a pad of paper and a pencil; I wanted to climb out of that rumble seat and make a weedy nest in the middle of the field, where I would sit for hours transcribing into words, for nobody but myself, the natural sounds I would hear, and everything I would see or feel in the moonlight, as if a holiness were there, in a landscape devoid of all human presence but my own.

That moment had become embedded in me, remaining

now as it had been at the time part of a desire to be free from any troubling social context. It is no wonder that the first words I managed to write in Florence constituted an exercise, an abstract essay on the effect of the natural cycles upon the psyche; that (whatever my dreams of Volterra) I was glad to be a stranger in Italy; and that the degree of my love for my fellows was in proportion to my remove from them.

Meanwhile, my wife and children were practicing a new language and beginning to make Italian acquaintances. It is difficult to remain a hermit in Italy—the people, the landscape, the climate, all conspire against it—, but what helped me more than benign surroundings to escape my cell was my growing acquaintance with T. through his letters and stories (I read several times the story about the ferryman Semyon)—and a particular expression on my son Cris' face. As part of his course in Renaissance art, he had gone with his instructor and classmates to the monastery of San Marco to view Fra Angelico's paintings, and had been so pleased by what he had seen and learned that he wanted to be guide and tutor for Jean and me on an identical tour of the framed paintings in the hospice, of the large fresco of the Crucifixion in the chapterhouse, of that of the Annun-ciation—considered that saintly painter's masterpiece—at the head of the staircase leading to the monks' cells, and of the series of small frescoes that Fra Angelico and his assist-ants had made, as encouragement to meditation, for each monk in his otherwise unadorned cell. I would find it im-possible to imagine any experience more harmonious with my wishes of that period than the actual tour of San Marco that Cris gave us; Fra Angelico's innocence, which enables a viewer to be ravished by something so simple and pure as the color blue, his painterly and spiritual desire to detach himself from all that is material and hence corrupt—in his "Last Judgment," he could paint the heavenly rapture on the faces of the saved but had to leave the faces of the damned to his helpers—held an enormous attraction for me. My son's face, though, held a greater one—the shy but radiant expression that first came to it in the hospice as he was trying to explain to us something he had learned about the twelve musical angels that frame the painting of the Madonna of the Guild of Flax Makers. His face made me conscious of those of others who also cared for what they saw.

A visitor to a foreign land is particularly sensitive to the accents of his countrymen, and to me American voices almost invariably sounded arrogant, slurred, and raucous. And yet, leaving San Marco, I lost my embarrassment at voices uncomfortably similar to my own in looking at the faces of men, women, and children—Italians, Germans, and Japanese as well as fellow Americans. A museum visit that includes a response not only to paintings but to people looking at them in wonder or love can transform, at least for a time, a person's apprehension of the wholly human world.

Later (this is one of the inescapable dangers of education), Cris' study of the more naturalistic and complex Masaccio diminished his enthusiasm for Fra Angelico; and I too came to prefer those painters whose works contain a greater struggle or tension.

12

T.'s joyful assessment of his countrymen upon crossing the river—"My God, how rich we are in good people!"—was accompanied almost at once by the renewal of his curiosity in people who resisted that classification to one degree or another: a bragging and lying official, for example, with whom he shared a carriage, a drunkard who ordered others about but who nevertheless was surprisingly good-natured; a more depraved but equally drunken braggart, an exile who had lost an eye in a fight, who claimed to have been a merchant in Moscow, and who held in contempt those upon whom he depended for bread.

For if in some crucial way T.'s perception had altered, his eyesight was directed upon human and natural worlds that remained constant. He had perhaps four hundred miles of further mud to traverse—actually, the worst roads of the entire trip lay before him—and the dull landscape still stubbornly resisted any tokens of spring. He had many swollen rivers and streams yet to cross; from his various ferries he saw peasant women rowing toward flood-made islands, to milk the thin cows marooned there. One such crossing was particularly dangerous. Instead of the booming T. had heard on the bank of the Irtysh, there was an alarming crack of thunder—"A queer thing in a cold wind, with snow on the ground," he wrote—while the ferry, which was unusually long, was being loaded. It was the precursor of a storm that roiled the water as the boat floated over a meadow near some willow clumps. The ferrymen argued about whether it would be more hazardous to continue the crossing or to remain by the willows, hoping for a change in the weather before dark; they resolved their quarrel by voting, with the majority electing to proceed. If the idea of death no longer oppressed T., he could still be frightened by the untimely prospect of it: long afterward, the figures of other passengers—a small and fearful soldier, a rigid mail-driver—remained in his memory as a tableau, accompanied by the thoughts he'd had about flinging off his hampering clothes if the boat overturned in the frigid water.

Two days after leaving his land of happy people but only fifty miles beyond, he arrived in a major town of the plain, Tomsk, whose streets seemed but arteries for the mud oozing past shops and houses on its own mindless journey to the ever-receding horizon. No doubt it was a sign of his renewed self-confidence and belief in his ability to be shrewd and resolute that in Tomsk he bought a chaise of his own to carry him for the duration of his trip by land, to the steamer at Lake Baikal. The chaise was a poor purchase, however; it kept breaking down, and finally T. had to sell it at a loss. He confessed to a continuing incompetence in his dealings with others that led him to pay more than was necessary for goods and services.

Had he, then, changed at all? Physically, his health was better than it had been for years. Except for the migraine headaches brought about by the punishments he saw inflicted upon the prisoners on Sakhalin, he would have few bodily complaints until sometime after his return to Moscow. Still, his experiences in Tomsk suggest the precariousness of his spiritual recuperation in its early days, even though it was from his hotel room here that, recalling everything he had just been through, he wrote the long letters describing his exultation. What is evident to me is that his recovery required anonymity, a continued separation from his own past and his social identity. His fame, unfortunately, had reached even this outpost of civilization; arriving in town, he saw advertisements for performances of a one-act farce he had written. It had been reported to T. that the play had highly amused the Czar at a performance in his summer palace; T. himself referred to the farce as wretched and vulgar.

Forced by the floods to remain in Tomsk longer than he wished, he would have been content to rest in his room and catch up on his correspondence and the accounts of his travels he had promised Suvorin for his newspaper. The letters, though, frequently contain the notation *"Stop!"*— for he was interrupted by natives of the town come to pay their respects. The editor of the local newspaper was one, visiting for whatever he could gain for his journal and himself; obligingly, T. accompanied him to dinner and bought him one beer after another while listening to his boasts of sexual adventures. Another was the assistant chief of police, whose arrival was not only disturbing, but alarming to T.

As part of the preparation for his trip, T. had gone to Petersburg to seek authorization for the highly unusual visit to the State's most remote prison colony. He personally delivered a written request to the chief administrator of prisons, and the care with which he had phrased his brief note suggests his unease. "Planning as I am to leave for eastern Siberia in the spring of this year on a journey with scientific and literary goals," the statement read, "and desiring as part of this journey to visit the island of Sakhalin, both its central and southern areas, I am taking the liberty of most humbly asking Your Excellency to extend me all possible assistance in achieving the goals stated above." The administrator welcomed T. warmly and promised documents, but these were never provided; actually, the official had written to his subordinates on Sakhalin, warning them of the approaching visit and instructing them to keep T. away from certain political prisoners and exiles. T. therefore undertook his trip without authorization, and when a hotel servant came to his room to tell him that a police official was waiting to see him, his first thought was that an order had been issued for his arrest.

From the details he gives in the letter he was writing at the time, one can imagine a narrative of what then happened. Hurriedly donning his wrinkled frock coat, T. rushed to the tarnished mirror above the washstand to brush ineffectually at his tangled hair and wild beard, and was appalled to notice that both they and the scales on his face had given him the look of a convict or exile. By the time the policeman knocked sharply on the door, he had returned to his chair by the little table. He was relieved that his unfinished letter was to Suvorin, that prosperous conservative and publisher whose newspaper supported the state, and that his words contained nothing incriminating.

"Come in," he called, dipping his pen into the inkwell.

"My dear sir," the policeman exclaimed, embracing him. "What an honor!" He apologized for interrupting T. in the composition of what doubtless was another masterpiece. Sitting on the bed, he criticized the hardness of the mattress as if it were partly his own fault—"Oh, our detestable town! No true comfort, no culture!"—and then, crossing his legs and twisting the tips of his mustache, declared not only his admiration of the work of T. and other great writers of the country but for that of the geniuses of France and England. He quoted a line from La Fontaine in French, and part of a soliloquy of Hamlet in a translation he declared to be his own and which, if rendered back into English, would begin something like this: "To endure as if in perpetuity or to snuff out the candelabrum of life is a conundrum of the first order."

"You are a writer, then?" T. asked.

"Only as a diversion. The plays I write are what our amateur theatrical troupe deserves, I'm afraid. It gives us all something to do that is different from the stuff of our lives and keeps me from blowing out my own dim candle." He spoke not only of the misfortune of being mired in a town that might as well be in the middle of one of the seas on the moon, but of his joyless marriage. His wife was as hateful to him as he unfortunately was to her; he had a mistress who also was caught in an incompatible marriage. "Why, my dear sir, are the laws we must obey so rigid that we can't live openly and in perpetuity with those we love?" he asked earnestly, jumping from the bed to stand before T. "Why should our government prevent us from divorce, if husband and wife alike fervently desire their freedom?" He gave T. a look of sly or abashed daring. "Pardon me, but did you possibly bring some vodka from Moscow? The local kind smells like piss and rots the liver."

T. offered to go downstairs with him for a beer in the hotel restaurant or a nearby tavern. "I accept," the policeman said, smiling radiantly. "And while we're there, you might as well look over my latest play. I'll be right back with it." Looking at T. as if for approval while dashing toward the door, he stumbled against a leg of the bed. "Oaf," he said to himself, and was gone.

T. barely had time to write Suvorin that his alarm at the sudden intrusion by the assistant chief of police had been wholly unnecessary before his visitor returned, breathing hard and tidying his hair in the mirror much as T. himself recently had done. Although he had brought his manuscript, his courage had left him. "Garbage," he said of it, and read instead a copy of a petition for divorce he had addressed to the Czar, one obviously written with all the care of T.'s request to the chief administrator of prisons and containing a self-conscious literary flourish. The policeman tucked the petition into a pocket. "This town has absolutely no facilities suitable for eminent guests," he said. "Drinking beer in the tavern would be boring. The best I can offer in the way of entertainment is the brothels. I go in my official capacity, so you have nothing to fear. But I must warn you that with one or two exceptions you won't find the women attractive. Would you like to go?"

In the edition of T.'s letters I read in Florence, the one written to Suvorin from the hotel in Tomsk has a series of periods—the indication of an ellipsis—soon after the particular "Stop" occasioned by the return of the assistant chief of police. The censor in this case was the English translator; a more recent edition includes the reference to the policeman's offer to take T. on a tour of the whorehouses and contains the words, "Am writing this on coming back from the brothels. Disgusting. Two A.M."

But whatever sexual desires might have been aroused by his new physical well-being, I find it inconceivable that T. would have selected a whore that night. Prostitution aroused in him a sense of revulsion. Young men in Moscow often made the rounds of the brothels, dancing with the prostitutes to the music of small orchestras and drinking with them, but not necessarily buying any further services. As a medical student, T. and two fellow students once visited the Moscow prostitution district to make—this is the reason he gave in a letter—a scientific study of the "unfortunate slave women," a visit that ultimately resulted in a story. The main character is a law student of romantic and idealistic bent, a talented youth who has an extraordinary empathy with the suffering of others; but he himself suffers from a self-constraint that leaves him less open to experience than are his friends. Trying to overcome this deficiency (a motive that probably also contributed to his author's willingness to undertake his brothel study), the law student accompanies two other students on a trip from bordello to bordello, but becomes increasingly horrified by the degradation he observes, and by his sense that the men who buy these short-lived and already spiritually dying or dead women are responsible for killing them in body and soul. Much as did T. in his investigation, the law student questions the prostitutes, trying to discover the nature of their lives and what led them to sell their bodies. His friends pay for bedroom visits while he waits outside in the snow. As soon as they rejoin him, he tells them they are murderers; one of them angrily responds that there is more vice in his look than exists in the whole street of whorehouses. Unable to discover any action of his own that might ameliorate the condition of the whores or put an end to prostitution, he becomes tormented and ill, as if it is he who has been victimized; his mental anguish becomes so severe that he no longer cares for the welfare of the women or of anybody else, and has a breakdown.

In tagging along with the policeman from brothel to brothel, T. no doubt joined his guide in consuming much cheap alcohol. However, if the policeman, with an appealing or sheepish look back at him, did finally ascend the stairs with a woman, T. would have remained at his table, staring at his glass of vodka. Whatever made him agree to a night of such entertainment? Perhaps he went from a feeling of relief that this provincial representative of authority had not arrested him, even though his motives for going to the penal colony included ones that any despotic regime would recognize as subversive to its authority. Perhaps he went because of his empathy with the policeman, who was himself trapped by autocratic rules and who was offering the only kind of hospitality he could think of. In traversing half a continent, T. had overcome much within himself; nevertheless, all that can be said with certainty from his experiences in Tomsk is that he was not yet sufficiently free.

In one of his last letters before leaving the town, T. dismisses this particular accumulation of buildings and people with his old refrain that in his country all towns are alike; but as he traveled onward beyond the rain and snow and mud into a land with blue skies and evergreen forests and lovely river valleys and attractive communities nestled beneath mountains, it was the vile Tomsk that he constantly used for contrast, as if its mire and dung constituted the whole of a civilization he finally had left behind.

III

In a New World

13

In beginning my account of T.'s journey, I found myself enjoying the task of imitating his narrative manner, as I constructed from whatever facts I had a series of tales about that social identity he was escaping or reforming. As he has been traveling eastward, though, I have found an ever-lessening need for those fabrications that reveal a social or psychological truth. Fiction feeds on the impurities of human relationships, the very impurities from which T. has been fleeing; and now he must get his definition elsewhere. As a child, how intently I listened to the voices, fading and then strong, sometimes obscured by radio crackle, of a Lowell Thomas in Tibet, an Admiral Byrd at Little America, a trapped Floyd Collins speaking into a microphone dropped into his Kentucky cave! An elemental truth about man and nature was transmitted by those solitary voices; and, particularly after Tomsk, it is much the same with T. Here, for example, are some words of his:

. . . From Tomsk to Krasnoyarsk was a desperate struggle through impassable mud. My goodness, it frightens me to think of it! How often I had to mend my chaise, to walk, to swear, to get out of my chaise and to get into it again, and so on! It sometimes happened that I was from six to ten hours getting from one station to another, and every time the chaise had to be mended it took from ten to fifteen hours. From Krasnoyarsk to Irkutsk was fearfully hot and dusty. Add to all that hunger, dust in one's nose, one's eyes glued together with sleep, the continual dread that something would get broken in the chaise (it is my own), and boredom. . . . Nevertheless I am well content, and I thank God that He has given me the strength and opportunity to make this journey. I have seen and experienced a great deal, and it has all been very new and interesting to me not as a literary man, but as a human being. The Yenissey, the Taiga, the stations, the drivers, the wild scenery, the wildlife, the physical agonies caused by the discomforts of the journey, the enjoyment I got from rest—all taken together is so delightful that I can't describe it. The mere fact that I have been for more than a month in the open air is interesting and healthy; every day for a month I have seen the sunrise.

T. wrote these words on June 5 in a letter from Irkutsk to Nicholas Leykin, the editor of a comic magazine. Leykin had published T.'s stories in those early years when he wrote simply as a means of earning a livelihood. Much of this work was trivial and formulaic, and T. considered some of his contributions to the magazine as so much shit. ("Excrement" is the word in the biographies; T. preferred a commoner scatology.) Although he wrote flattering and even obsequious notes to Leykin—as a young writer who had won no prizes he had not yet squeezed the serf out of himself—he distrusted him as an editor and disliked the vulgarity of his journal. Long before undertaking the trip, T. had come to resent Leykin's patronization of him, as if his success were wholly the consequence of the editor's discovery and promotion of his talent; in turn, Leykin had been angered by T.'s decision to send his stories to magazines with higher literary standards and pay scales, an action Leykin felt to be a betrayal of trust. Why, then, would T. write him now, and again a few weeks later, as if they were nothing but old friends? Partly, I think, because in his attempt to gather enough cash to finance his trip, T. had asked Leykin for whatever royalties had accumulated on an early collection of his work and Leykin, impecunious though he always pretended to be, had sent him in advance of the proper date the requisite small amount. And because, as the letter indicates, his anomie had vanished, taking with it all vestiges of bitterness.

How agreeable it is to accompany an ever-happier T., one whose journey each day took him farther from the sloughs of despond! Nearing Krasnoyarsk, he found both the weather and topography to have undergone a miraculous transformation: he descended from chill woods onto a dry and grassy plain with grand mountains in the sunlit distance, and birch trees in full foliage. Krasnoyarsk, a town of paved streets, large stone houses, and handsome churches, was nearly surrounded by walls of mountains rising into the mists; through the valley flowed the broad Yenissey, a river that to him was far more beautiful than the Volga. He felt that he had entered an entirely new world, so picturesque and serene that it struck him as odd that his government sent people into exile here.

If Tomsk was the last outpost of the old world, Krasnoyarsk was the first of the new. Beyond the town and its river was the wilderness of the taiga—an unbroken coniferous forest that continued for a full thousand miles. None of T.'s drivers knew how far north the forest went, or what existed within it; in winter, a driver told him, stangers

from the arctic regions traveled the taiga, bringing or following reindeer, which they bartered for bread. They came
from, and vanished into, the silence. Whenever his road
reached a summit, T. could see only thickly-forested
mountains and occasionally the dust from another carriage
either proceeding or following his chaise. Ever since leaving Tomsk, he had been more or less accompanied by two
lieutenants and an army doctor who were traveling to a
remote post on the Amur River. These soldiers would have
been a protection had brigands been lying in wait around
some curve. . . . T. felt the almost pleasurable fear one has
in uninhabited regions, those places in which the life one
perceives belongs to a mysterious animal gliding among the
boles in a dark green shade; but he was glad of the solitude.

At the post stations, as well as in the hotels at either
end of the taiga, his military companions were so fiercely
aggressive that innkeepers and waiters were afraid to present them bills for service: "In their company," T. wrote,
"I pay less than usual." But he lost more than he gained;
they had gambled or otherwise squandered away the
generous sum for traveling expenses each had been given,
and so he lent them money. In the public baths at Irkutsk,
he washed off the accumulation of dust, smoke, and dried
facial scales; the brown color of the soapsuds (it was, he
said, as if he were washing a horse) undoubtedly came to
his mind as he wrote—much later, from the country estate
he purchased following his return to civilization—of the
dust-covered Alyohin's millpond bathing. Actually, it was
in Irkutsk that T. seriously began to contemplate the purchase of such an estate. He would put off all professional
ambitions for four or five years after his return, he decided,
in order simply to enjoy a personal existence; and so he
wrote to Mary to begin looking for a suitable home in the
country for the family. It delighted him to find in Irkutsk a
tavern named for that town by the southern sea in which he
had been born. Irkutsk had a comfortable hotel, a munici-

pal garden in which a band played, a museum, a theater, and cabs with springs; he was free to wander about, responding to these amenities like any tourist. And in Irkutsk he dreamed one night of the long-haired Lika, who was so much more beautiful than the local women.

By this time he was weary of his companions. "It is much nicer traveling alone," he wrote his sister from the hotel. "I like silence better than anything on the journey and my companions talk and sing without stopping, and they talk of nothing but women." But he had no good reason, after selling his chaise, for not becoming one of their party; and so all four rode in the same carriage on the short journey to Lake Baikal. In 1890, the mountainous shoreline was almost deserted and the water free of the industrial pollution which I have read has become a problem in recent decades: this deepest of all freshwater lakes, with a surface area nearly as large as Switzerland, has hundreds of inlets but only one outlet. In T.'s time, the road in winter continued across the ice, the distance being so extensive for horse-drawn vehicles that each season a post station was erected in the middle of the lake; by June 13, the date T. arrived at the station on the shore, the steamer, of course, was operating. Driving on an exquisite day to the lake through a mountain valley, his route paralleling the wide river that was the outlet, T. felt, he said, "exceptionally well; I felt so happy that I cannot describe it." The scenery was "something new and original"—a phrase that was to become the leitmotif of the remainder of his trip to the island, even as "In Russia, all towns are alike" had been that of the earlier portion. "We drove along the river bank, came to the mouth of the river, and turned to the left; then we came upon the bank of Lake Baikal, which in Siberia is called the sea. It is like a mirror. The other side, of course, is out of sight. . . . The banks are high, steep, stony, and covered with forest, to right and left there are promontories which jut into the sea . . . ," and he began making

analogies between this area and that of southern seaside
resorts in which, even though the mountains were less
striking, life was particularly pleasant.

He wanted now so urgently to reach his goal on
schedule that the several days of waiting for an erratic
steamer temporarily made him lose his pleasure in the
natural loveliness. One day it rained; he was cramped with
his army companions in a small barn-like structure on the
shore. They continued to talk and argue; one of them was
an insufferable braggart whose posturing intensified T.'s
wish to be a solitary traveler. "To sit in a chaise or in a
room alone with one's thoughts," he wrote in a letter to
Mary from the shore, "is much more interesting than being
with people."

But his pleasure and sense of wonder prevailed. He
crossed the lake third class, on a deck chiefly occupied by
frightened wagon horses, whose kicking and neighing con-
trasted with the liquid stillness. The water was of a tur-
quoise transparency: looking into it to a depth of what he
was told was over half a mile, he saw rocks and mountains.
The beauty and threat of that submerged world "sent a
shiver all over me. Our journey over Lake Baikal was won-
derful. I shall never forget it as long as I live." Language is
apt to result in such clichés whenever words grapple for a
beauty too deep for any human ordering. Reaching the
other shore, he and his companions galloped on, now cov-
ering well over a hundred miles each day. Writing to his
mother of the final days of his travels by carriage, he said
that part of the trip, along the banks of a river, had been
"one continuous loneliness" but that in another part he
"found everything" he ever had desired: for it carried to his
mind, as one experience of *déjà vu* after another, all the
landscapes that had delighted him since childhood, reality
becoming one with the imagination of it.

His three-thousand-mile horse journey ended exactly
two months after it started on the day (it was June 20) that
he reached the river port of Sryetensk, just over an hour

before his steamer was to depart for the last leg of his trip across a continent. Despite everything he had endured, he had kept to a schedule he had calculated from his combination doctor's office and writer's study in Moscow. That success elated him. "I wish nothing better for anyone," he wrote. "I have not once been ill, and of the mass of things I had with me I have lost nothing but a penknife, the strap off my trunk, and a little jar of carbolic ointment." He bought a first-class ticket because his companions bought second-class ones, and he wanted to be separated from them by at least a deck.

Sometime after returning home, T. summarized his adventures in crossing a continent by remarking that he saw prose before Lake Baikal and poetry afterwards. Once aboard the river steamer, though, he found the poetry to be changing: a romantic awe before natural spectacles that intensify the need for, and pleasure in, solitude gradually became a more social idyll of the kind one can have on a cruise that combines all the creature comforts of civilization with stopovers at various exotic and primitive ports.

The difference of the shipboard experience is first suggested in a change in his attitude toward his former companions. No doubt it was guilt on his part that made him search the second-class deck for them; he found the two lieutenants, and invited them for tea. One of them he now discovered to be modest and well educated; T. felt he could have traveled with him "for a million versts without becoming bored." The other, the braggart, remained impossible, but even he was found to have a redeeming quality, a perhaps excusable excess—a fondness, like T.'s, for babbling on about relatives. A stronger indication of the difference in T.'s attitudes comes from what at first seems the oddness of several of his metaphors for a natural world that so recently had provided spiritual therapy. In voyaging down a narrow and turbulent tributary of the great river that would carry him to an ocean he had dreamed of while reading narratives of eastward journeys as a child, he found its banks to be "picturesque like stage scenes" that yet were "oppressive in this complete absence of human beings. It is like a cage without a bird."

The steamer continually tacked about, to miss sandbars and to avoid running into the bending shoreline. At one stop, a handful of convicts—no previous indication of their presence aboard exists in the letters I have read—disembarked, for nearby were a prison and mines worked by the inmates. At another stop, he wandered through the streets of a little town that was "nothing to boast of, but one could live there." Just as the perils of the tributary seemed over—at its juncture with the Amur, that major river which was the boundary between his country and China—the steamer hit a rock and foundered. The water being shallow, it didn't sink far, but it took over three days for the crew to patch the rips in the hull with greasy rags held in place by boards which in turn were kept firm by timbers wedged against the ceiling. Meanwhile, the ship blocked the channel; another steamer headed upriver was forced to wait. A military band aboard the other ship provided entertainment for passengers on both steamers, turning the waiting period into such a festival that T.'s crew lost its desire to go on with the repairs; even the captain became indifferent to the progress being made. T. asked a fellow passenger, "Whenever are we going on, do you think?" The other replied, "Aren't you all right, here?"

"Yes," said T., and laughed. Accompanied by the band, passengers from both ships trooped ashore, even though there was little to see in that military settlement. In mingling with the passengers, in talking with peasants and soldiers in the taverns, T. felt as if he might be in the American West. The inhabitants of the region—peasants, exiles, and priests alike—mined for gold, and talked constantly about that precious metal. Rich one day, they became such lavish spenders they soon were penniless. To his sister, he wrote of his astonishment at discovering people who look like laborers or craftsmen but "who never drink anything but champagne, and walk to the tavern on red baize which is laid down from their hut to the tavern."

Finally afloat again, the ship glided down the Amur. Through his opera glasses, T. observed the birds on the shore—enormous groupings of "ducks, geese, grebes, herons, and all sorts of creatures with long beaks. This would be the place to take a summer villa in!" He enjoyed the fact that the banks of the river were indistinguishable from each other, even though they belonged to separate nations, and that inhabitants of one could cross without hindrance into the land of the other. Everything struck him as original, but especially the people. He so loved the Amur, he declared, that he would be happy to float down it for two years. The society he found on its banks was the perfect kind for any sojourner who has been wandering in the wilderness long enough both to exult in his personal liberty and to wish for the solace of the human community—for the region was so removed from its source of authority that it was actually autonomous, free of religious and political proscription and the accompanying rigidity of caste and convention.

He wrote his sister that the inhabitants of these river towns "don't keep the fasts, and eat meat even in Holy Week; the girls smoke cigarettes, and old women smoke pipes—it is the correct thing. It's strange to see peasants with cigarettes! And what liberalism! Oh, what liberalism!" The people could speak openly of whatever they wished, for there was "no one to arrest them and nowhere to exile them to." If the administrators of the prison up-river were to overstep their authority, the entire Amur region would be in rebellion. "An escaped political prisoner can travel freely on the steamer to the ocean, without any fear of the captain's betraying him. This is partly due to the absolute indifference to everything that is done in Russia. Everybody says: 'What is it to do with me?'" To Suvorin T. spoke of the "beauty, space, freedom and warmth" of the Amur. "Switzerland and France have never known such freedom. The lowest convict breathes more freely on the Amur than the highest general in Russia."

At Blagoveshchensk, not quite halfway down the Amur, he had a layover, necessitated by his transfer to another steamer. Did he have to change ships because the rags of the first were no longer adequate to the task of holding back the water? To me, those rags serve as well as anything else to represent the careless freedom, or nonchalance, that T. liked about the people on this river.

As far back on his journey as Irkutsk, he had met Chinese; and now, having penetrated deeply into the Orient, he not only was surrounded by Chinese but saw many Japanese—"or, to be more exact," as he explained to Suvorin, "Japanese women, petite brunettes with large, complicated hairdos, beautiful torsos, and, as I had occasion to observe, low-slung hips. They dress beautifully. Their language is dominated by the sound 'ts'. . . ." This particular reference is missing from that early volume of letters I read in Florence; of the two more recent translations, one carries the letter to the above point, while the other adds one more sentence following a still-expurgated passage: "The Japanese girl's room was neat, asiatically sentimental, and cluttered with bric-a-brac. . . ." In its false juxtaposition, the sentence makes the preceding "ts" sound like a censor's cluck of reproof for whatever it was that he expunged.

And so the reader, like T. himself in Blagoveshchensk, has the freedom to follow his or her own fancy, given only the restrictions imposed by the knowledge of T.'s character. The Japanese girl most certainly would not have been a prostitute. Was she perhaps a waitress he met in a restaurant, a servant in his hotel? I think not. Nor do I imagine her a geisha—a girl to be hired for her culture, her conversational ability at dinner, and her attractiveness—though I admit this as a possibility. I consider her as fairly well-off—a young woman who has come to Blagoveshchensk for an extended stay to regain her independence of spirit

(however barbarous the town's name, a more suitable environment for such a recovery would not exist) after her
Tokyo lover betrayed her for a marriage to a woman with a
greater dowry; perhaps a grandson of this shrewd marriage
now is the wealthy manufacturer of video games exported
to America. Never mind that my conjecture ignores any
Japanese conventions of the time concerning arranged mar-
riages; I wanted T. and Olga to make love on the Volga for
both their sakes, but knew that such a consummation was
then highly unlikely, and now I would provide a love affair
of an ideal sort. To me, the jilted girl is a painter whose
talents far exceed those of Sophia Kuvshinnikov, whose
husband gave T. that flask of brandy which yet lies unopened in his luggage. When T., descending the gangplank
of his rusty and doubtlessly sinking ship, first sees her, she
has set up her easel on the riverbank to paint the docks, the
haze over the water, and the opposite shore—that far edge
of a nation alien to them both but soft in the radiance of a
late-afternoon sun which touches them as well. He admires
her painting, and tells her that he has tried his hand at
charcoals and watercolors, without much success; but that
the talent for painting runs in his family—his sister paints,
and he had a brother, Nicholas, with an extraordinary gift
for it, a brother whom he loved but who died too soon.

Does she, this Japanese girl, understand a word he
says? She understands his eyes, certainly. "Ts, ts, ts, ts,"
she responds, laughing, and dabs a bit of color from her
brush on his wrist. That evening they bathe in the pure and
warm Amur (a river that a Russian couple now exiled in
my upstate New York community pronounce as if it were
identical with the French word for love), drink champagne
at a candlelit dinner, and so to bed. If censorship prevents
me from knowing what truly took place, I am, like Juliet's
nurse, happy with my imaginings of it, as pleased by the
simple fact of T.'s love-making as I was depressed to slog
with him through the mud. In Florence, even though I was
ignorant of this brief romance, I was much the same kind

of emotional sponge, absorbing T.'s despair before the accident with the mail carts and the slowly-intensifying pleasures after it.

On his new and watertight vessel, T. completed his river voyage. His stateroom companion, a happy and pigtailed Chinese, told him, before falling into opium-induced dreams, that in the land he came from one's head was chopped off for the most trivial of infractions. The stateroom glowed with fireflies, a new phenomenon to T.: "Meteors are flying in my cabin," he wrote to his sister. "Wild goats swim across the Amur in the daytime. . . . Little by little I seem . . . to be stepping into a fantastic world." Upon awakening, his Chinese companion "began to sing from music written on his fan."

By the time the steamer reached Nikolaevsk, its terminus, the weather had turned cold and rainy. The town was still on the river, but was the port for ocean vessels; here T. transferred to the liner that would take him across the straits to Sakhalin. On this ship, which was named for that lake that had transformed his trip into poetry, he saw a convict with fetters on his legs who was accompanied by his daughter, a girl about six. The father, T. learned, had murdered his wife. T. watched as the child held her father's chains while he climbed the stairs out of a latrine.

T. never mentions the moment at which he consumed his brandy.

14

The villa in which we had our apartment was the central building of a compound, a little world. In the gatehouse lived a friendly peasant couple who told Jean and Cris—it was during one of their first attempts to carry on a dialogue in Italian—that they never had been outside Florence. They were proud of their son; from the time of his early childhood, he had been interested in tennis because of the proximity of the courts on the via Michelangelo, had once won a tournament in Bologna, and now, married and with a child of his own, was a tennis instructor. During the year of our stay in the villa, the son bought a new Fiat *cinquecento* and one Sunday took his parents on a drive to Siena. The car, which the parents washed and polished afterwards, was a far greater marvel to them than their escape to another city. Another peasant couple—a rougher and more taciturn pair whose world, so far as I could tell, never extended beyond the gatehouse and who seemed still to be existing in the middle ages—lived in the combination barn and farmhouse behind the villa, separated from it only by a rear courtyard. A Peruvian sculptor kept a studio in a former storage room of the villa; he gave lessons in sculpting to Jimmy and the two sons of the villa owners, who lived on the ground floor. Our landlord was a professor at the University of Florence, married to an Englishwoman. Though he spoke little English, the children were bilingual; the boys, a mischievous pair roughly Jimmy's age, at once made friends with him by introducing him to their method of augmenting their allowances. Putting on their most tattered clothes and smearing dirt on their cheeks, they took up a position on the nearby via Michelangelo, and in a mute and imploring fashion held out wildflowers (as well as flowers from their mother's garden, if she weren't there to protest) to the German and American tourists passing in their cars.

Her years in Italy had given our landlady a fine Italian nonchalance before whatever is unavoidable in life. She read a good deal—mainly English novels, even though the attitude of writers from her native land toward the inhabitants of her adopted country was one of the few things that infuriated her. "Oh, those restrained, *rational* English!" she once exclaimed to me, holding her hand palm-up and shaking it. "They think Italians are good for their souls because to them Italians are instinctive, like animals."

Most of the apartments in Florence or Rome that are available to foreigners are burdened with an excess of furniture and ornamentation. Ours, though, had no pictures and was sparsely furnished with old chairs and tables taken at random from various rooms of the villa—a fact that pleased all the members of my family, for it enabled us to treat the apartment as if it were our own home. A dealer in antique furniture for export, an Italian who was the father of one of Jimmy's classmates, told us that our dining-room chairs were sixteenth-century French; he was horrified to discover that beetles were dropping sawdust from tiny holes in the legs and seat frames. Our landlady, who refused to be bothered by possessions, was vexed by our news the following day that the chairs were both valuable and beetle-infested. "But what is one to do?" she asked, and immediately changed the subject by encouraging Jimmy and Cris in their idea of painting a mural on the whitewashed kitchen wall. Still under the influence of Fra Angelico's musical angels, Cris painted an elaborate border which, however, predominated not in angels but in oak and maple leaves. In the foreground, as the first image of the mural itself, appeared a long and slender body of water, a representation of that Finger Lake nearest our country house outside Ithaca; and beyond it there soon stretched hills of an ambiguous nature—Tuscan? Upstate New York? Future generations of art scholars could decide. Rows of olive trees sprouted full-grown on these hills, and cypresses outlined the horizon. The cow of the nursery rhyme jumped over a moon originally intended as the sun; by the shore a fanciful version—for the horses were unicorns—of the carrousel that belongs in Ithaca's lakeside park awaited the approaching children. One morning I discovered that a fair facsimile of the engaging octopus that swims beside the boat of the three Magi in one of the mosaics of the baptistry on the Piazza del Duoma was floating in the blue waters of Lake Cayuga.

On the day we packed our belongings—including a wooden sculpture the Peruvian artist had made—into our car to begin our homeward journey, we embraced, with all the fervor of natives, our landlady, her children, the gatehouse couple, and the artist. Our landlady told us that whoever rented our apartment would have to accept the mural, for never would she allow it to be touched. She was a genuine Italian at that moment—one to whom the truth of emotion displaces all considerations of practicality or future fact. A student of mine, visiting the villa the following year, found out that the mural had been painted over at the request of the new tenant.

Not everything about our year's residency in the apartment was harmonious. Our landlord—he had inherited the villa, but left the details of its operation, including the renting of the apartment, to his wife—disliked us, or at least remained distant, always formal and correct, for we were Americans, and hence implicated in the atrocities still occurring in Vietnam. The peasant husband who lived in the farmhouse had a rabbit hutch near his courtyard door; Jimmy liked to pet the fat little animals, and one day brought a schoolmate to see them. The peasant chose that moment to kill one of the rabbits by driving a pointed stick through its eye and into the brain—and the memory of that action and of the rabbit's frightened shriek tormented Jimmy at night for weeks. He did not manage to maintain his early friendship with the boys whose villa it really was; a rivalry that in the end amounted to enmity developed between them.

And yet that year gave both my wife and me the openness to experience that people can have who are far enough from home to ignore their duties as citizens and who have no need to concern themselves with the problems of their host country. One evening our landlady telephoned Jean from police headquarters, asking her to tell her children that dinner would be late, but that they shouldn't worry—their father was all right, and would be released from jail.

"What happened?" Jean asked. The landlady said he had been clubbed by the police and charged with sedition for his participation in a demonstration in front of the American consulate. Italian justice being what it was, he might have been imprisoned for months or even years while awaiting trial; but fortunately, the right lawyer had contacted the right official. . . . It was not unknown in America, of course, for demonstrators to be clubbed, but it would have been remarkable for one of them to be charged with sedition—or for any person who was accused of an offense against the state to be so quickly forgiven. Whatever had happened was beyond our experience; we

shrugged like Italians and put it aside as an oddity of behavior in a volatile but endearing land. Equally strange was
the fact that one of Cris' Italian acquaintances, an obviously intelligent young man from Sicily, belonged to the
Fascist party.

"Why?" we asked him, rudely enough, during his
only visit to our apartment. He said that Sicilians who
valued freedom tended to be Fascists, because Fascists
were the only ones who had ever had success in opposing
the tyranny of the Mafia. "Visit Sicily," he said. "The people are very poor, but nobody would dare to steal a camera
from the car of a tourist—the Mafiosi don't permit petty
crime."

In winter, Florence becomes cold and rainy; and so,
during the Christmas school vacation, we did take a trip to
Sicily, driving the autostrada south. Evidently Italians
don't travel at Christmas time, for often we were the only
guests at a hotel and restaurants were frequently closed. If
no restaurant in a given town were open, somebody would
direct us—once by motorcycle—to the nearest place where
meals could be had. On Christmas Eve, we cajoled a family
who ran a trattoria in a village near Potenza (searching for a
hotel, we had strayed from the autostrada) to serve us at
least spaghetti, though they were in the process of closing
to ready themselves for the religious services; they were so
pleased by our appreciation of their spaghetti sauce that
one by one additional dishes appeared—sausage, veal,
salad—, and soon all the members of the family were sitting with us. As we were finally leaving, they gave us
special pastry to eat on Christmas morning.

The farther south one goes on the autostrada, the
more one rides the ridge of the Apennines; the highway
becomes a series of prodigious engineering feats occasioned
perhaps by a desire on the part of the government to avoid
offense to those on either the right or the left of that rugged
spine. The interchanges are curving sculptures suspended
above one abyss or another by legs that seem too slender to

withstand any new tremor of this presently-dormant vol-
canic land; the soaring concrete is brave in its graceful
acknowledgment of transience, and hence has a beauty not
found in the ancient Roman aqueducts.

I was thinking of such airy matters—in particular, of
the relationship of art to attitudes about the future, including eternity—when we entered a snowstorm that belonged
in upstate New York. We were alone on this magnificent
but slippery highway on Christmas Day; if the car went
over a bank, nobody would witness the accident. Far off,
over a snow-covered plateau, I saw a desolate village
nestled on the slope of a mountain. It was the kind of
primitive settlement, perhaps, that T. had now and again
reached, prior to the poetry of Lake Baikal, and in similar
weather. Unlike T., we had a heater and were protected by
metal and glass. Unlike his journey, ours would be both
brief and festive. Why should I have felt the appeal—it was
so intense that I can still recapture it on this windy October
day nearly thirteen years later, looking out my study window at colored leaves skittering across the road and at a
field whose recently-sprouted winter wheat makes it as
green and tidy as any park—of that remote hamlet on a
mountain slope, a scattering of houses whose combined
value, at least in dollars or lire, was far less than that of the
nearest interchange?

Perhaps it was something as simple as fear that made
me want to be in that village instead of on a highway
become surprisingly treacherous. And it is true that even as
relative affluence and comfort can make distant poverty
seem picturesque and enticing, so the awareness of familial
love—of the mutually-protective companionship contained within the fragile shell of a moving car—can give a
husband and father an openness to the silence and re-
moteness that is, if not the antithesis of, certainly the end
to, a wholly human love. In any event, I was glad to reach
the interchange at which we left the still-uncompleted
autostrada for a road that slipped off the mountains into

the warmth below; and glad to reach a Sicily fragrant in the sunshine with the smell of oranges. Those succulent blood oranges of Sicily—the best the world provides—were being hauled to market by horse-drawn wagons and by trucks, their beds piled so high that a slight bump could make fruit drop off, to decorate the shoulders of the narrow roads. If we wanted oranges, we could slow down, open the car doors, and swoop them up.

We spent a week on the island. At a seafood restaurant in a fishing village at the base of Mount Etna, we looked from our open-air table at the oddly-shaped boulders in the harbor, which, according to local legend, the blinded Cyclops had thrown in his rage at the escaping Ulysses and his crew. I suppose thousands of tourists before us had wondered, as we did, whether Etna itself could have been the rock-throwing Cyclops, a fissure his cave, and a fiery vent his eye. To discover a possible natural cause for our distant ancestors' wonder permits a mythic event to be re-experienced in our own less credulous minds.

While looking at the ruins of the Greek colony at Agrigento, we learned from our guide that not earthquakes but Christian righteousness had tumbled the pagan temples, still beautiful in their hint of a past spiritual ordering of stones. Although we had come to Sicily to view the classical sites, I remember most strongly the people, like that guide—a man dressed as neatly as his tattered suit would permit. Intelligent, proud in his knowledge, he took us on a tour more extensive than the customary one, but would accept no additional fee for the hours he spent with us. Agrigento is a reputed Mafia stronghold, but certainly his conduct—his kindness and his interest in us—was a personal matter. Early one afternoon we stopped in a village in the interior—yet one no more than a half-hour's drive from Taormina, that tourist mecca—to buy food and drink for a roadside lunch. The street was deserted, but I stayed in the car with our luggage while Jean and our sons entered a store. Almost at once, men in pairs were walking toward the car, their eyes averted until they passed; in the mirror, I could see them quickly look back. Crossing the street at the corner, they returned on the opposite dirt path, far enough away from the car for them to look directly at me and for one or two to wave. Meanwhile, women as well as men crowded into the little store to watch Jean select her items, with solicitous advice from the shopkeeper. *"Tante grazie,"* Jean said; and all the onlookers smiled broadly and replied in chorus, *"Prego."*

The Sicilian dialect is distinct from the Florentine Italian that Jean and the boys were learning in their separate schools; but they—and even I, to a lesser extent—were able to communicate with the woman in Piazza Armerina who, having prepared and served us food, sat down with us, as had the family on Christmas Eve. We were in her previously-closed restaurant at the insistence of a young man who had seen us wandering the dark streets, vainly searching for a place to eat. He had led us to hers, which was locked, and knocked vigorously on the door until she opened it. At first she was reluctant to admit us, for her husband, who did the cooking, was ill; but once she had invited us within, she became more and more hospitable. On a shelf near our table were several hand-carved models—souvenirs, for the tourist trade—of the traditional Sicilian peasant carts painted with scenes from Ariosto's *Orlando Furioso* and pulled by horses ornamented with plumes, tassels, and bells. Fascinated by the intricacy of models which might somehow be edible—for this was, after all, a restaurant—Jimmy asked the woman if they were made of chocolate. She hugged him, pleased by a question asked in Italian. "No, no," she said, and impulsively snatched one up and placed it in his hands. In the car, we saw from a tag that the little wooden cart and horse, for which she had refused payment, was priced higher than what she had charged us for our meal.

How does one account for this Sicilian generosity? I

had observed nothing like it in Florence or at home. Do culture, education, and wealth—or, for that matter, a baffled awareness that a nation's promise of opportunity and equality is at odds with the social reality—narrow one's sympathies? Few Americans would want to live in a Sicilian town or village—the rigidity of conventions, the inequality between the sexes, and the general oppression (whether imposed by poverty, church, or Mafia) would infuriate us. I tried to be realistic in my assessment of all the kindnesses offered us, knowing that in part I was responding to a change in my own awareness. The people we met and talked with obviously were better off than the peasants we saw cooking their evening meals on braziers set in the narrow space between the road and their hovels. And even these selected people we met—did they treat each other as they treated us, a family from an exotic land? It was impossible to tell; and so I simply accepted the fact of my happiness with them.

On our last day on the island, noticing that we were almost out of fuel, I stopped at the first station I saw. Set on a barren hill, it consisted of a single, hand-operated pump and, for an office, a wrecked Fiat placed on concrete blocks. The elderly attendant waited for customers in one front seat, his dog in the other. While that wrinkled little man filled our tank, I petted the dog, a curly-haired white animal of mixed breed that I praised—my knowledge of Italian adjectives limiting me to extravagance—as "intelligent" and "beautiful" because she licked my hand, barked vigorously, and wagged her tail. After we had paid for the gasoline with tourist coupons, the man brushed at the bugs on the windshield with a cloth—ineffectually, for his station had no water. He smiled at us, but seemed distracted; he motioned for us to wait while he searched first his pockets and then the Fiat. That search—motivated by the Sicilian desire to give—was in vain; he had nothing but his grimy cloth. Shrugging, he put it in my hand; and it was in my suitcase aboard the airplane that flew us to New York that summer. Also in that suitcase was the completed manuscript of a novel I had not expected to write, but which I had begun immediately upon our return to Florence from that holiday trip.

15

Snakes of fire—those cold flames nearby and in the distance—had been part of T.'s understanding of death in those moments following the collision of the mail carts, when he had felt nothing but his absolute isolation in an underworld of bitter shades. Later another fire blazed at the edge of the continent as the ship bearing him to Sakhalin moved into the straits. T. describes that fire in an early passage of his book about the island. A forest was burning, a layer of black smoke hanging over that "dense green mass" belching its "scarlet flames. . . . The conflagration was enormous, but all around was quiet and tranquil; nobody cared that the forests were being destroyed. Obviously the green wealth belongs to God alone."

The view clearly was disquieting to him. It was at once a natural phenomenon and a mirror of his psyche, reflecting his spiritual desire—for surely his wish for a freedom beyond self attracted him to that empty and serene forest in much the same way that it drew him to vistas of sky,

mountains, or water—as well as his old fear of those an-
nihilative forces that would consume not only the body but
all human meaning. The line that separates the creative
impulse from the destructive, the wish for selflessness from
that for extinction, infinite value from despair, is as tenu-
ous and thin as it is crucial. Augustine, aware of how an
impulse toward self-martyrdom can be mistaken for a love
of God, was instrumental in effecting the Catholic proscription against suicide.

T.'s arduous journey had prepared him, as fully as was
possible, for the suffering and degradation to be found in
the prison colony, but it would of course be misleading to
say that he had become impervious to psychic horrors and
doubts about human purpose. Nothing we have intensely
sensed, while awake or while asleep, is ever lost, no matter
how much we would later reject it as irrational or hal-
lucinatory; the very act of its burial in the memory makes it
more firmly part of whatever it is we are, and it will assert
itself unexpectedly, when we are fatigued or unwary. It is
possible that the black shroud of smoke T. saw on the
disappearing mainland resonated against his past nightmares. Did he see in it his eyeless bull's head, now
wreathed in black smoke—as he was later to describe its
appearance before one of his characters? I also connect that
black pall with a powerful and disturbing story he wrote
four years later, in the aftermath of a dream that might
have marked a new stirring of the illness his journey had
temporarily stayed. In the story, that dream—the image of
a black monk with a pale and emaciated face emerging from
a huge cyclone of smoke—is given as the recurring hallucination of a neurotic and increasingly deranged scholar. His
ability to perceive such a figure convinces the scholar that
he is extraordinary, one of God's elect; at the story's end
the monk metamorphoses out of his towering black pillar
to bring the scholar an ecstatic death.

Even one who has come to feel an intimacy with T.
from knowledge of his life and work is apt to be surprised

by this narrative's barely-disguised evocation of its author's psychic polarities. The monk first appears to the
scholar in a moment of solitude as the latter is walking
toward "a wide field, covered with young rye not in
flower. The distance held neither a human dwelling nor a
living soul, and it seemed that if one followed the path it
would lead one to that same mysterious and unknown
place where the sun had just sunk and where the sunset
now glowed with such imposing grandeur." It is a moment
that strikes the scholar as "spacious and free and peaceful."
Hence the monk is token of that quest for freedom which
will provide the soul with its desired truth and purity, that
quest which the pilgrim undertakes to release him from
anxieties about his mortality, reputation, and station in
life. The monk is also death, a figure to be welcomed only
by those who have gone quite mad. As the interpretation
of an ambiguous dream that doubtless both fascinated and
horrified T., this story is the only one of his I know of that
seems to have been composed, consciously or not, as an act
of personal therapy, that therapy proceeding from his
post-Sakhalin awareness of the dangers of a spiritual nar-
cissism.

What excited me most, in the conception of the major
and minor journeys that constitute my account, was the
possibility that at the very end I might be able to fuse both
stories, or subsume mine into T.'s, in language belonging
wholly to him. In bringing T. from his home in Moscow to
these straits between the continent and Sakhalin, I have
become increasingly dependent upon his own words, as
found in his letters and in those stories that reveal something about both his experiences and the inner nature of the
man who underwent them. I am glad that from this point
forward even the slightest invention is unnecessary. In his
book about Sakhalin, and in the story he wrote on the way
home, T. tells us all that we need to know.

IV

At the Penal Colony

16

At nightfall of his third day at sea, T.'s ship cast anchor, there being no harbor, at the mouth of a river on the island; on the following morning he was to disembark for the major post of the penal colony, Alexandrovsk, a town of three thousand inhabitants. The first view he had of his goal was one of further huge fires. "I could not see the wharf and buildings through the darkness and the smoke drifting across the sea," he writes, "and could barely distinguish dim lights at the post, two of which were red. . . . On my left monstrous fires were burning, above them the mountains, and beyond the mountains a red glow rose to the sky from remote conflagrations. It seemed that all of Sakhalin was on fire."

Shortly before the ship had reached this destination, an army officer in charge of a detachment of soldiers asked T. about his mission on Sakhalin; upon learning that he had come of his own volition as a civilian engaged in research, the officer showed surprise, saying that only government officials had permission to visit the island. The words depressed T., who had come so far, and who had never received written authorization for a stay on Sakhalin. Nevertheless, he had no difficulty the next dawn in reaching the shore; he left the ship with other passengers in a cutter that was towing two barges of silent convicts. The morning was sunny, with no hint from the land of the Hades he had observed the previous night. Nobody greeted or questioned him at the pier; he strolled about, wondering what he ought to be doing. As he passed a group of some fifty convicts, they removed their caps in unison. In recollecting this act of homage—a requirement of all convicts in the presence of authorities and other free men that he came to detest—T. remarks, "It is possible that no writer has ever previously received such an honor." The first acquaintance he made on the island was a self-important official who introduced himself as a collegiate secretary; they walked together for a time. T. asked what he might expect to find at the post, and the official sighed—ominously, it seemed to T.—and said, "You will see!"

Ultimately, he was able to get a carriage. He didn't know if it were possible for him to rent a room; the driver—a convict, for he took off his cap—assured him that it was, and drove him along a wholly civilized road, with curbs and street lights, to a house in the suburbs without ever entering the central part of town where the prison stood. How strange the ordinary can seem, to one who has expected the bizarre! The house itself was spacious and clean, though devoid of furniture. After showing him his empty room, the landlady left, to return later with a table, then a stool, and then tea. She wondered at his reason for visiting "this godforsaken hole." She herself had come as a young woman with her mother, who had followed her convict husband; now she—the daughter—was married to a much older man who, although he had grown rich through real estate and other ventures since completing his prison term, was gloomy and ill. . . . Out of T.'s window he could see nothing but cabbage sprouts, ditches, and a withered tree.

At noon, not knowing what else to do, T. took a leisurely walk through the streets of the suburb. He dawdled in a little shop which sold an odd assortment of merchandise—stars to be fastened to epaulets, Turkish delight, saws and sickles, and ladies' summer hats advertised in a handwritten price list as "very fashionable"—, and was invited by the owner to come to his house next door for a meal, an invitation that T., being hungry, readily accepted. The shopkeeper's house contained Viennese furniture, an American music box, and flowering plants. His host was a former officer of the guard who had been convicted of murder in Petersburg twelve years before, had completed his sentence, and now, in addition to profits from his shop and other business, received a governmental salary for overseeing road construction; his wife, who belonged to the nobility, had accompanied him to Sakhalin, and now served as a doctor's assistant in the prison hospital. Four other guests, all officials, had already arrived; they included a gray-bearded and elderly doctor who reminded T. of the playwright Ibsen. Dinner included soup, chicken, and ice cream; the beverage was wine. The guests spoke of politics and patriotism, and everybody except the physician praised the island. T. has recorded a portion of the conversation:

"When, roughly, was the last snowfall?" I asked.
"In May," the shopkeeper replied.
"That's a lie, it was in June," said the doctor who resembled Ibsen.
"I know a settler," said the shopkeeper, "who had a twentyfold yield from California wheat."

And again there was an objection from the doctor: "That's a lie! Your Sakhalin yields nothing. It is a cursed land."

"However, permit me," said one of the officials. "In '82 there was a fortyfold wheat yield. I know this for a fact."

"Don't believe it," said the doctor. "They're pulling wool over your eyes."

Before the gathering dispersed, the doctor told T. of a legendary curse put upon the island by a shaman of one of the indigenous tribes displaced by the arrival of the first Russians. "And so it has come to pass," the doctor said, with a sigh. Later in the day, T. discovered that the doctor had just been dismissed from his post, having so infuriated the island commandant in an argument about the condition of some incoming livestock that the latter had threatened him with his stick. Perhaps sensing in the newcomer a fellow malcontent, the doctor invited T. to stay in his house on the post's main street, near the prison and the business district.

T. moved in that evening, and thus never had to sleep in a room that lacked a bed. In the morning, he woke to the clang of chains and the sound of musical instruments. The street was filled with convicts, some fettered, who were engaged in preparations for a rare visit by the highest official of the region, the Governor-General, Baron Korf. They were building a new bridge over the river, constructing arches, painting buildings, sweeping the roads, carrying wheelbarrows of fresh sand to pour on the square before the commandant's residence. Horses trotted back and forth, perhaps learning parade behavior from their drivers. The sound of musical instruments came from the barracks across the street: the army band was practicing marches. "The flute played passages from one song," T. writes, "the trombone from another, and the bassoon from still another, and the result was inconceivable cacophony."

Cacophony—or at least an inability to make order out

of a bewildering variety of sense impressions—seemed to be what T. first suffered from on the island. Although the opening chapters of his book reveal little of what he was to discover, his hindsight imposes upon his early impressions an ironical awareness, as if he were detached from this naive and curious newcomer. Initially, he reminds me of a character in a work of fiction—not so much his own as a novel by that Polish-born contemporary of his, Conrad. T. is a Marlowe, aware of dark portents and hints while being exposed to festivity, culture, and people with the best of intentions.

Granted interviews first with the island commandant, General Kononovich ("I'm glad you are staying with our enemy," that general said, referring to the doctor. "You will learn our weak points"), and then with Baron Korf, T. found both of them obliging, even supportive of his research. Evidently they felt there was nothing to conceal from him. They granted him permission to enter all the prisons and settlements and even, as if a freedom-of-information law existed in this most secluded of prisons in one of the most autocratic of states, access to all official documents. The only restriction—and it was not strictly enforced—was that he could not speak with political prisoners; this was a consequence of that missive from the state administrator of the prisons. In turn, T. was open and honest with them, declaring that he had neither an official assignment nor one from a newspaper or scientific society. It gave him, I think, a sense of his own integrity to refute suggestions that he might have a motive beyond purely personal ones for an investigation of the penal colony, even though some sort of institutional connection would have imparted a greater credence to his research.

T. liked General Kononovich, finding him intelligent and well-read and experienced at prison management. "He speaks and writes beautifully," T. reports in an early chapter, "and gives the impression of being a sincere man with humanitarian aspirations. I cannot forget how satisfied I was with our conversation and how favorably I was impressed by his aversion to corporal punishment." Baron Korf made time for a second and more lengthy interview with T., despite his official duties—he was kept busy on his brief tour watching the parades in his honor, tasting prison food (fresh meat was served the inmates, also in honor of his visit), magnanimously ordering the chains removed from a number of prisoners, listening to reports of the lesser administrators as well as petitions from convicts and such aggrieved free men as the recently-discharged doctor, and giving short speeches. ("I am convinced that the 'unfortunates' live better on Sakhalin than in any other place in Russia or even in Europe. In this area, much still remains to be done, for the road to kindness is an endless one.")

At that second interview, Baron Korf suggested that T. title his proposed study of Sakhalin "A Description of the Life of the 'Unfortunates,'" and dictated to him, for that description, some of his views about the prisoners. T.'s book contains the following words of the Governor-General that he obediently took down: "Nobody is deprived of the hope of enjoying his full rights; there is no such thing as perpetual punishment. Penal servitude for an indefinite period is limited to twenty years. Convict hard labor is not onerous. Forced labor gives no personal advantage to the workers; herein lies its burden, and not in physical exertion. There are no chains, no guards, no shaved heads."

No chains? Did Baron Korf, who had just ordered a few shackles struck off, believe that none remained? No guards? Who, then, were those people with uniforms and weapons? The hope of regaining full rights? Convicts who completed their terms before dying could become settlers, but were forbidden ever to return to their homelands. In writing his book, T. knew this quotation to consist of nothing but falsehood, but at this early point he only says of the baron, "From our previous conversation and from his dictation I received the impression that he was a magnanimous and honorable man, but that the 'life of the unfortunates' was not as well known to him as he thought." T. respected the commandant more than he did Baron Korf; and so, later in the book, after a discussion of the frequent and often sadistic flogging of convicts, he relegates to a footnote this comment:

> The present island commandant, General Kononovich, has always opposed corporal punishment. When the sentences handed down by the police administration and the Khabarovsk court are shown to him, he usually writes: "Agreed, except in the matter of corporal punishment." Unfortunately he has rarely enough time to visit the prisons and does not know how frequently the convicts are beaten with birch rods. This may be happening 200 or 300 yards from his headquarters, and the number of corporal punishments inflicted can be judged only by the reports on his desk. One day when we were sitting in his drawing room, he told me in the presence of some officials and a visiting mining engineer: "Here on Sakhalin corporal punishment is almost never inflicted; it is astonishingly rare."

Like cultured and decent people in oppressive circumstances elsewhere—Conrad depicts many of them, and doubtlessly they existed in the more terrible concentration camps of the next century and still do in the prisons of brutal regimes—, these two administrators maintained their idealism and self-respect through paperwork and illusion. They also were prisoners of a larger social structure, one with a willful ignorance and a desire to maintain the political and judicial status quo—an insight that T., in order to get his book past the censors, could only hint at. In their first conversation, General Kononovich told him, "Everyone tries to escape this place—the convicts, the settlers, and the officials. I have no desire to escape yet, but already I am exhausted by the great amount of mental exertion demanded of me," and the captain of the ship that brought T. to the island said of himself and others in an official capacity, "We are the prisoners, not the convicts."

The so-called collegiate secretary, T.'s first acquaintance, was another who, caught in the prison net, lived by his illusions. He thought of himself as a poet, and often accompanied T. on his sojourns, reciting his latest verse as they walked. Although "collegiate secretary" apparently was his civil service designation, he actually served as a prison guard, and referred to his duties as those of a "director of labor and laborers." He so respected such titles that on one occasion he screamed at a woman who made the mistake of referring to him by name instead of calling him "your excellency." The illusions of the penal colony were, in fact, a magnification of those of the larger society from which T. had wished to escape; and if he were, indeed, engaged in scientific research, the colony was a laboratory in which he could assess such abstruse subjects as human meaning and the health of his own soul.

If one does not wish to be but another character in an elaborate social fiction, one must somehow get at the underlying facts. T.'s book is weighted with statistics of value to historians and social scientists and geographers, as well as reformers who need figures for evidence. It is documented with careful observations made as he traveled from prison to prison, from settlement to settlement, bearing with him the census cards prepared for him at the police department print shop that gave him his excuse for brief interviews with ten thousand "unfortunates." Work helped to rescue him from his feeling of being merely fictive. But the appalling truth of the book is finally a moral one. The direction of the inner journey about to begin is implied in a pair of descriptions at the end of the prologue to his investigations.

The first conveys the fantasy and charades of the unreal world, and the second another kind of fantasy altogether, for it communicates nostalgia for a recollected reality and permits T.'s initial understanding of, and perhaps spiritual identification with, a convict. The first depicts festivities occasioned by the visit of the Governor-General; the second a carriage ride during which T. and his convict driver come upon another convict propelling a cart down the railroad tracks with a pole, much as a ferryman would pole a barge across a dark river:

1.

There were illuminations during the evening. Until late at night soldiers, settlers, and prisoners milled around in throngs along the streets lit with lamps and Bengal lights. The prison was open. The Duyka River, always pitiful and dirty with its bleak and barren banks, was now decorated on both sides with multicolored lanterns and Bengal lights, and their reflections in the water were lovely that evening, majestic and ludicrous, like a cook's daughter dressed up in the gown of her employer's daughter for the purpose of a fitting. Music was being played in the general's garden, and there were singers. They even shot off the cannon, and the cannon burst.

2.

The days were beautiful with a bright sky and clear air, reminiscent of fall in Russia. The evenings were magnificent. I remember the glowing western sky, the dark-blue sea and a completely white moon rising over the mountains. On such evenings I enjoyed driving along the valley between the post and the village of Novo-Mikhaylovka; the road is smooth, straight; alongside are rails for mining carts, and a telegraph line. The further we drove from Alexandrovsk, the more the valley narrowed, the shadows deepened; giant burdocks began to resemble tropical plants; dark mountains closed in from all sides. In the distance we could see the flames from coke fires, and there were more flames from a forest fire. The moon rose. Suddenly a fantastic scene. Coming toward us along the railway was a convict, riding in a small cart, dressed in white and leaning on a pole. I feel terrified.

"Isn't it time to turn back?" asked my convict driver.

Then he turned the horses, and glancing up at the mountains and the fires, he said:

"Things are boring here, your excellency. It is much better at home in Russia."

17

In the eastern portions of the Russian Empire, now the USSR, lakes and islands are as big as many nations elsewhere. If Lake Baikal is nearly the size of Switzerland, the island of Sakhalin, as T. says to give his readers a geographical measure against which to compare it, "is twice as large as Greece and one and a half times the size of Denmark." In width, it varies from about a mile and a half to eighty miles; two mountain ranges, separated by a valley, run for most of its six-hundred-mile length. In T.'s time, the northern section was not colonized, its harsh climate and unproductive soil—permafrost is found there—precluding agriculture of any kind. Two major penal districts existed, each with its towns and villages and prisons—one in the central portion of the island, with Alexandrovsk as its administrative headquarters, the other in the south, with Korsakov as its main post.

How does one investigate such an expanse of land and

settlements, giving order and unity to his findings? T. had simply his census cards. He spent two months in Alexandrovsk or its vicinity, visiting the prisons and then individual houses of penal colonists in the various settlements, some of them difficult to reach because of poor or nonexistent roads in the mountainous interior. Later, fatigued not only from the physical hardship but from what he had witnessed, he traveled by ship to the southern region of the island to repeat the cycle. On his census cards, he recorded the name of each convict or settler interviewed, his or her address, status, age, religion, birthplace, principal occupation, marital status, education or degree of literacy, and— for those who lived in the settlements—the amount of prison assistance received.

Of course, he learned much more from his encounters than the statistics reveal. One of his biographers refers to the remark of an observer, perhaps the guard who sometimes accompanied him, that T. so readily gained the trust "of even the most hardened criminals" that they spoke openly to him of their lives and feelings. And among the papers left at his death are a number of letters written to him in the years after 1890 by convicts who wanted to keep in touch with him. Still, the statistics themselves—the very listing of persons, their religious preferences and native provinces—are an affirmation of the value of individuals. The prison records were inadequate; the names of many prisoners and former prisoners become settlers, and the children born to them before and during their exile, had been garbled or lost or never noted. During his sea journey to the southern region, T. had leisure, at last, for a few letters; in one to Suvorin, he wrote with pride of his statistics, and said, "I was particularly successful with the census of the children, on which I am building great hopes."

To T., the children offered the chief resource for combating the drift toward bestiality and hopelessness, the erosion of self-dignity, decency, love, and, indeed, the obliteration of the very sense of selfhood imposed by conditions of life on the island, both in prison and out. He recognized the degree to which the children on Sakhalin were exploited, often by their parents. On an Alexandrovsk street, he met a sixteen-year-old girl who had been a prostitute since she was nine; he heard of a mother who operated a brothel in Alexandrovsk, using her own daughters as whores. The small food allowance granted by the prison for each child often bought the father a bottle of contraband vodka or gave him money for gambling at cards, which provided the convicts' chief entertainment, other than sex.

T.'s book on Sakhalin is written in the first person, a mode he normally did not use in writings intended for publication; although on occasion the book reminds me of James Agee's *Let Us Now Praise Famous Men*, a first-person account of experiences with white tenant farmers in the South during the Depression, T. avoids as best he can the subjectivity that was so crucial to the later writer. Agee shies away from the issue of his tenant families' attitude to the Negro poor, perhaps because it would be an impurity in his empathy with the whites, an impediment to his own guilt—as an educated and well-fed person—for their sufferings. But if T. dismisses or bypasses anything about his convict families, I am unaware of it. The stupidity, cunning, or coarseness he observed on the faces of many of his convicts, whether they had committed serious crimes or not (some were apparently the victims of judicial errors and others were undergoing a lifetime of suffering for a youthful desertion from the army) are faithfully described, as are the acts of violence, including murder, that some of them continued to commit. The animalistic aspect of faces no longer haunted him as a mirror of his own fear of human meaninglessness; he simply recorded what he saw. And whatever his sympathies for the very young and their parents, he recognized that "the birth of a new child in a family is not accepted joyfully. Lullabies are not sung over the cradle. . . . The fathers and mothers say that they cannot feed the children, that they will not learn anything good on Sakhalin, and 'the best possible fate for them will be if the good Lord takes them away as soon as possible.' If a child cries or is naughty, they scream at him maliciously, 'Shut up; why don't you croak!' "

And yet the small children "bring an element of tenderness, purity, gentleness and joy into the most calloused, morally depraved Sakhalin family." Collecting information about a three-year-old boy, T. "said a few kind words to the child," whereupon the father, who had been indifferent, apparently lost in his despair, became suddenly radiant and nodded his head in happy agreement with T. "that his son was a very nice little fellow." While interviewing two women who had followed their convict husbands to the island and who shared the same house, he observed that one, who was childless, was consumed with a hopeless grief—she never should have come to Sakhalin, she told T. bitterly, in front of her husband, whose expression revealed guilt for her anguish; the other woman, mother of several children, looked on silently, displaying none of the childless woman's nervous mannerisms or her self-reproach that reached out to indict another.

The children on the island, T. observes, "are pale, thin, and flabby. They wear rags and are always hungry." Their mortality rate was, of course, high. Some of them lived in the prison barracks, sleeping on the single continuous plank bed that served all the convicts—usually, but not always, men—and their families. The prison atmosphere influenced even the games the children played on the streets: some of them pretended to be soldier guards, others convicts who, if they escaped, were to be caught and whipped. The sight of fettered prisoners was so commonplace the children were indifferent to it; T. saw several of them laughing uproariously as they held onto the back of a wheelbarrow of sand being pulled by a chained prisoner.

From his census, T. determined that 2,122 children, "including adolescents who became fifteen years of age in

1890," lived on the island. He knew with certainty that 644 of them had accompanied their parents to the colony, and that 1,473 had been born either on Sakhalin or during the long trek to it. There were only "five children whose place of birth I do not know." It is remarkable that T. was able to collect such apparently precise statistics. Traveling from settlement to settlement, he did not allow the appalling conditions he saw—the filth, including human excrement, everywhere; the lack, sometimes, of a well, which meant that the settlers had to get their water from ditches; the undernourishment and starvation that led a number of these supposedly self-supporting agricultural colonists to eat the seeds allotted them for planting as well as their pitiful beasts of burden—to interfere with the accuracy of his record. In a hut in one settlement, he found at home only a ten-year-old boy whom an American reader could imagine as a Tom Sawyer or a Huck Finn—he was a freckled towhead, and barefoot—were it not for what he revealed to T. in the interview:

> I: What is your father's patronymic?
> He: I don't know.
> I: You live with your father and you don't know his name? Shame on you.
> He: He's not my real father.
> I: What do you mean, "not real"?
> He: He's just living with ma.
> I: Is your mother married or widowed?
> He: She's a widow. She came here for her husband.
> I: What is "for her husband" supposed to mean?
> He: For killing him.
> I: Do you remember your father?
> He: No, I don't. I'm a bastard. Ma gave birth to me on the Kara.

What possible value did T. find in his patient recording of statistics about all these deprived and sometimes spiritually maimed children? For one thing, the numerical accounting gave at least a sense of the magnitude of the problem. The food allowance—a niggardly sum—provided by the prison administration for child support masked that problem, by implying a concern for the welfare of the children on the part of a bureaucracy that was actually indifferent to what the money was used for. In a footnote, T. says:

> If it were up to me, I would use the money now distributed in "food allowances" to build teahouses at the posts and in the settlements for the use of all the women and children. I would distribute food and clothing rations to all pregnant women and nursing mothers without exception, and I would only reserve the "food allowances" . . . for distribution to girls from thirteen years old and until they are married, and I would have this money given to them directly.

This last suggestion obviously was intended to save the girls from the prostitution they were forced into simply to survive.

In this lengthy footnote, T. also outlines a program not unlike some adopted by philanthropic organizations of our own day: he would institute an annual report containing detailed information similar to that provided by his census, and this information would be made available to citizens who might wish to help these malnourished and otherwise underprivileged children. "If, for example, a philanthropist knows how many children can read and write, he will then know how many books or pencils to send so that no one would feel hurt by being left out. He could ascertain the number of toys and the amount of clothing necessary if he knew their sexes, ages, and nationalities."

Following his return to Moscow, T. led a campaign in which several thousand volumes were collected for use in the schools on the island. The publication of his Sakhalin manuscript—most of it serialized in a journal in 1893–94, the book in its entirety available in 1895—created a considerable interest in what had been an obscure penal colony. Donations, mainly for the welfare of the children, came in; the government sent two officials on an investigative mission to the island. One woman is known to have left for Sakhalin to devote her life to the prisoners and their families; whether, given the grim circumstances of existence there, particularly for women, she maintained her courage and nobility of will, I do not know.

Did T.'s book make a more significant impact than this? Bureaucracy, perhaps in Russia even more than elsewhere, is a cumbersome machine, and only in 1903, a year before T.'s death, did the government legislate against the head shaving, the flogging, and the chaining of prisoners to wheelbarrows in the Far Eastern penal colonies. T.'s book must have played a part in these and other reforms; the last-named punishment, administrated only on Sakhalin, certainly had been brought by him to public attention. The following year, the penal colony itself was done away with; war—between Russia and Japan—was the reason, though the act was in keeping with what is apparent from T.'s book: that the major solution to the problem of suffering on Sakhalin would be to abolish the use to which the island was put. Intended as a self-sufficient agricultural colony, Sakhalin had a climate and a soil that made such a goal absurd except on paper, a fact that T. quickly came to realize; so far as he could determine, only one area could reasonably be expected to support a colony. The officials compounded the problem by selecting locales for the settlements on the basis of administrative convenience rather than suitability for human living; and they continually subdivided the available parcels of land into ever smaller ones to accommodate each new influx of hungry and wholly unprepared colonizers.

Censorship, as well as his own temperament, kept T.'s

book from becoming rhetorical, but its facts and level-headed observations contain one indictment after another. The most obvious, since it is the most bluntly stated, concerns the operations of the coal mines at Due, the original post of the colony, and the one with the most antiquated barracks and prisons. In every respect, Due and its surrounding settlements in the somber and narrow valleys provided "the most horrible and hopeless" environment on the island. Here the floggings were most brutal; here the living conditions the filthiest and most sordid. Here one cold and gloomy morning T., in the company of a prison physician, saw an old man prostrate on the sand by a sea whose waves frothed and thundered against the rocks; two other convicts knelt by him, helplessly holding his hands. T. suggested that the victim be given "at least some valerian drops," but his companion said the prison "had no medicine whatsoever," and so the two of them walked on.

In the mines at Due, the convicts, many of them fettered, worked as long as they were able to dig and carry out the coal in carts, but the profits all went to a private corporation—maybe "five people" in faraway Petersburg—that provided absolutely nothing, not even a mining engineer, for the supervision or improvement of the facilities, and of course paid nothing to their laborers. T. quotes an official report as saying that the whole operation "has 'all the earmarks of plunder,'" and he remarks that the administration, in permitting the continuance of such profiteering while ignoring the abysmal conditions it engenders, "sacrifices the aims of reform to industrial considerations, which means that it is repeating the old mistake, one which it has always condemned."

His remarks on the abhorrent Due are as close to muckraking as his book gets. Nevertheless, he manages to imply an additional severe charge: that the colonization of the island has led, through exploitation and the introduction of infectious diseases, to a gradual, though unwitting, genocide of the indigenous population. The early intruders

from Russia had subjugated the inhabitants by treating
them as though they were the convicts to come, by tying
their hands and then whipping them, or sending them
fleeing to some remote section of the island. T.'s encounters with members of the various tribes provide a counter-
theme to the major theme of brutality, ignorance, and
injustice; for these native peoples were gentle and responsible and extraordinarily truthful. On one occasion, he met
two members of the Gilyak tribe, who assumed he was a
clerk (a *"pishi-pishi,"* in their fractured or pidgin Russian, a
phrase that roughly translates into English as *"writee-
writee"*) because, as always, he was carrying paper for his
notes and census-taking, and who asked him (such frankness being their customary approach) how much money he
earned. Answering them with a corresponding truth-
fulness, T. gave them an approximation of his monthly
income as a writer. Both of the men, he writes,

> suddenly grabbed their stomachs, and bending to the
> ground, they began to sway as though they had severe
> stomach cramps. Their faces expressed despair.
> "Oh, how can you talk that way?" I heard them
> say. "Why you say such an awful thing? Oh, that's
> bad! You shouldn't!"
> "What did I say that was bad?" I asked.
> "Butakov, the regional superintendent, well, he's a
> big man, gets 200, while you are not even an official—
> you just write a little and they give you 300! You
> speak badly! You shouldn't!"
> I tried to explain that a regional superintendent re-
> mains in one place and therefore only gets 200 rubles.
> Although I am just a *"writee-writee,"* I have come a
> long way—10,000 versts away. My expenses are
> greater than Butakov's and therefore I need more
> money. This calmed the Gilyaks. They exchanged
> glances, spoke together in Gilyak, and stopped suffer-
> ing. Their faces showed that they finally believed me.

"It's true, it's true!" said the bearded Gilyak briskly. "That's fine. You may leave now!"

"It's true," nodded the other. "You may go!"

Whatever their attributes (including a refusal to be awed by authority) that particularly appealed to him, T. was unsentimental about these people. He observed that members of the tribes did not believe in washing, that their hovels exuded a dismal stench, and that the males in at least one of the tribes treated their women as chattel.

Mistreatment of women, though, was not limited to the indigenous population. In previous years, before the institution of certain reforms, the arriving female convicts had been immediately placed in a house of prostitution; if they refused or did not "earn" the favor of the guards and administrators, they "were forced to work in the kitchen." According to a report from that pre-reform era, those who became prostitutes generally also became drunkards, "so depraved and stupefied that 'they could sell their own child for a pint of alcohol.' " Commenting elsewhere in his book about the reforms that have come to the colony, T. says, "Times have changed. Young officials are now more common than old ones, and should an artist portray a scene showing a prisoner being flogged, the painting would depict an intelligent young man in a smart new uniform instead of the former old drunken captain with a purple nose." That new enlightenment brought a similar change in the disposition of women convicts. No longer were they put at once into a brothel. Instead, "they are accompanied ceremoniously" from the ship by officials, and followed by clerks, guards, and settlers looking them over—a scene that T. found analogous to a run of spawning herring being pursued by "platoons of whales, seals, and porpoises" that would feed upon them. The youngest and most attractive of the women became servants of the officials, who had first choice; those slightly less desirable were consigned to "enter the harems of the clerks and guards"; and the majority of those remaining became cohabitants of the more prosperous and influential settlers. A typical response of a female convict, once an agreement with a man had been reached, was the cautious question, "You won't mistreat me, will you?"

As for the "free" women—those who had voluntarily come, often with their children, to be with their husbands—, they were apt to end up in one of the communal barracks, sleeping with their husbands and children on the same plank bed that served other convicts and their families, while "a piglet wanders around the ward and slobbers; the floor is covered with slimy muck, the ward stinks of bedbugs and something sour. . . ." The "disrespect and contempt" given women and children were nowhere more evident than in the "barbaric" wards at Due, where "fifteen- and sixteen-year-old girls are forced to sleep beside convicts."

The communal wards were at the heart of a system that, ostensibly concerned with the reformation of character, led to a further corruption of it. The lack of privacy and the general degradation of course appalled T. Returning to prison after a day of work in rain or snow, a convict would have to use some of his damp clothing as bedding. "He has not had a bath for a long time, is full of lice, smokes cheap tobacco, and constantly suffers from flatulence. . . . He squishes the bugs on the plank bed with his fingers." Inmates stole from each other; acts of violence, often connected with gambling at cards, included murder. Such crimes went unpunished, for the guards were corrupt and, for a bribe, would look the other way. A convict infrastructure, a kind of Mafia, existed within the communal wards; it was headed by prisoners who had created a monopoly in the sale of provisions (bread, sugar, tobacco, alcohol) to their fellows, and who, with the assistance of brutal pawnbrokers, controlled the gambling operations.

The miasma of spiritual as well as physical decay was absorbed by those administrators who, unlike the idealistic commandant and others whose duties kept them out of the prisons, were unable to maintain their distance from it. Soon after their arrival on the island, these civil servants, members of the intellectual class, became aware of their "complete helplessness to combat the encompassing evil," and slowly became a part of it. They began to steal and to enjoy the sadistic whippings that at first had horrified them. T. met one official who boasted that he had cured the prisoners of the habit (particularly prevalent among those in chains) of presenting "absurd petitions." He had whipped the majority of them for submitting requests and complaints that in his judgment were not justified, and now was no longer bothered by petitions of any kind.

His need to observe and report on all activities at the colony led T. to witness a flogging at Due of a prisoner who had been caught while trying to escape the island. His capture had caused the authorities to notice that they had forgotten to punish him the previous year for the murder of a Cossack and his two granddaughters; he was to be given ninety lashes for that offense and, upon recovering, would be flogged a second time for his attempt to escape. T.'s description of the punishment is as precise and impartial as he can bring himself to make it. The executioner "pulls down the prisoner's trousers to his knees and slowly ties his hands and feet" to the flogging bench.

"Brace yourself!" he says softly, and without any excessive motion, as though measuring himself to the task, he applies the first stroke.

"One-ne," says the warden in his chanting voice of a sexton.

For a moment Prokhorov [the convict] is silent and his facial expression does not change, but then a spasm of pain runs along his body, and there follows not a scream but a piercing shriek.

"Two," shouts the warden.

The executioner stands to one side and strikes in

such a way that the lash falls across the body. After every five strokes he slowly moves to the other side and the prisoner is permitted a half-minute rest. Prokhorov's hair is matted to his forehead, his neck is swollen. After the first five or ten strokes his body, covered by scars from previous beatings, turns blue and purple, and his skin bursts at each stroke.

After "a peculiar stretching" of the victim's neck and "the noise of vomiting," T. found himself unable to watch; he walked out to the street, returning to witness only the last blows of the leather-thonged lash.

Prokhorov's hands and feet are quickly released and he is helped to his feet. The flesh where he was beaten is black and blue with bruises and it is bleeding. His teeth are chattering, his face yellow and damp, and his eyes are wandering. When they give him the medicinal drops in a glass of water, he convulsively bites the glass. . . .

"I love to watch them being punished!" the military medical assistant exclaims joyfully, extremely pleased with himself because he saw his fill of the abominable spectacle. "I love it! They are such scum, such scoundrels. They should be hanged!"

18

One settlement on the island reminded T., as he crossed the "splendid wooden bridge" to enter it, of the "real" villages of his distant homeland; less cramped and much more picturesque than any other he had found in the colony, it didn't give the impression of being forced by edict upon a hostile site. Willows grew on the stream banks; the settlers' huts, each with its well-tended garden, faced wide streets; and the prison compound—the prison itself was new, and around it were a scattering of tidy buildings, including the warden's house—resembled less a place of confinement than a baronial estate. What an antithesis to the bleakness and horror of Due! Clanking his keys as he went from one warehouse to another, the warden was "exactly like a landlord in the good old days who guards his stores day and night. His wife sits near the house in the front garden, majestic as a marquise. . . . There is a feeling of quiet contentment and ease." Like the warden and his wife, the convicts whom T. first observed—the warden's gardener, his wife's dressmaker, the fishermen netting salmon in the stream for the prison officials' dinner—"walk softly like cats, and they also express themselves softly, in diminutives: little fish, little cured fish, little prison rations. . . ."

It is of course impossible for any reader—or for the writer himself, for that matter—to identify all of the experiences and feelings that lie behind a specific literary work. I believe, though, that T., in dreaming up at his country home that story in which the veterinarian Ivan tells of his fat brother's contentment on his estate, the story that makes Ivan appalled by the very idea of happiness, was influenced by his memory of a prison compound like a nobleman's estate, one whose serenity depended upon an absolute disregard of what existed not only within the prison, but a short distance from the central streets, where half the populace was "starving, in rags, and . . . hardly alive." No village of his homeland, not even one recently ravaged by fire, presented, he felt, such disparity between well-being and misery.

The warden gave him comfortable enough quarters for the night in a new warehouse on the prison grounds in which, strangely enough, Viennese furniture was stored. It was raining. T. stayed up until 2:00 A.M., copying data for his census and reading. As a modern critic suggests in his introduction to the translation of T.'s book, what happened during the dark hours of the night and in the early daylight must have inflicted upon T. the most despairing and oppressive effect of the entire experience of Sakhalin:

> The rain fell continually, rattling on the roof, and once in a while a belated prisoner or soldier passed by, slopping through the mud. It was quiet in the warehouse and in my soul, but I had scarcely put out the candle and gone to bed when I heard a rustling, whispering, knocking, splashing sound, and deep sighs. Raindrops fell from the ceiling onto the latticework of the Viennese chairs and made a hollow, ringing sound,

and after each such sound someone whispered in despair: "Oh, my God, my God!" Next to the warehouse was the prison. Were the convicts coming at me through an underground passage? But then there came a gust of wind, the rain rattled even more strongly, somewhere trees rustled—and again, a deep, despairing sigh: "Oh, my God, my God!"

In the morning I went out on the steps. The sky was gray and overcast, the rain continued to fall, and it was muddy. The warden walked hurriedly from door to door with his keys.

"I'll give you such a ticket you'll be scratching yourself for a week," he shouted. "I'll show you what kind of ticket you'll get!"

These words were intended for a group of about twenty prisoners who, from the few phrases I overheard, were pleading to be admitted to the hospital. They were ragged, soaked by the rain, covered with mud and shivering. They wanted to demonstrate in mime exactly what ailed them, but on their pinched, frozen faces it somehow came out false and crooked, although they were probably not lying at all. "Oh, my God, my God!" one of them kept sighing, and my nightmare seemed to be continuing. The word "pariah" comes to mind, meaning a person who can fall no lower. During my entire sojourn on Sakhalin only in the settlers' barracks near the mine and here . . . on that rainy, muddy morning, did I live through moments when I felt that I saw before me the extremes of man's degradation, lower than which he cannot go.

If their requests for hospitalization had been granted, the convicts' health might have improved as a consequence of the reprieve from labor, but certainly not as a result of medical care. Before leaving the island, T. visited one of the newer prison hospitals. On a bed lay a convict who had attempted suicide by slashing his throat, and from the wide gash T. could hear air escaping, as he breathed; the wound was untreated. The dressings on the patients recovering or dying from surgery were filthy. Except for a convict who once had been a medical assistant, the hospital attendants were untrained and surly. T. himself decided to lance an abscess on the neck of a young boy; the scalpel given him being blunt, he requested another, which turned out to be just as dull. The assistants had difficulty in locating the carbolic acid—it was obvious that they rarely, if ever, used it—and were unable to provide a basin, cotton, decent scissors, or even sufficient water.

It is no wonder that T.'s experiences on Sakhalin began to give him migraine headaches, depression, and new nightmares. During his excursion to the southern region in his last month on the island, T. visited a site, overlooking the ocean, that had once contained a military post. Nothing remained of that settlement. In his book, he attempts to recollect the feelings he had at that moment, and to me the description is a companion piece, as much an answer as his soul could then offer, to the human degradation he had sensed as, coming out of the warehouse, he had seen the prisoners standing in the chill morning rain and miming their ailments:

> The sea looks cold and murky. It roars with fury, and the high gray waves rush up on the sand as though saying in despair, "God, why did you create us?"
> This is the Pacific Ocean. On this bank of the Naybuchi can be heard the sound of the convicts' axes at the new building site, and on the other shore, which can only be imagined, is America. To the left through the fog you can see the promontories of Sakhalin, to the right more promontories . . . and not a single living soul around you, not a bird, not a fly. For whom do these waves roar, who hears them during the night, what do they want, and finally, for whom will they roar when I have gone away? On this shore

you are gripped not by thoughts but by meditations.
It is terrifying, but at the same time I want to stand
here forever and gaze at the monotonous motion of
the waves and listen to their ominous roaring.

Like his fiction and plays, the emotional strength or
meaning of the book comes less from its "story" or narrative movement than from its combinations and large struc-
tural arrangements. The last four chapters, which were
banned by the censors in the manuscript's first publication
as magazine serialization, contain intriguing relationships;
taken as a whole, they constitute for me (as apparently for
the censors) the essential attitude of the book—a way of
looking that makes of convicts, settlers, guards, and
officials a single human unit, a grievously-flawed society
which inevitably reflects the greater one beyond it. Although they deal with extremity of behavior in a given time
and place, these chapters are sufficiently universal to apply
not only to the present-day Soviet Union and other repres-
sive regimes but in a measure to that far-off America which
came to T.'s mind as he stood on the fog-enshrouded
Sakhalin shore, looking over the Pacific Ocean.

The subject of the first of these final four chapters is
the "free" population of Sakhalin—the soldier-guards, the
clerks, the intelligentsia—, showing them all caught in the
net which the opening has foreshadowed. The society is
demoralized; on paper, a theoretical apportioning of responsibility exists, but in practice—because of ignorance,
stupidity, hardships, inefficiency, corruption, and a contempt on the part of some of these "free" people for each
other that is obvious to the convicts they would reform—
the society lacks the moral or ethical base necessary for its
implementation. T., that great exponent of personal freedom, here perceives the need for an adequate social organi-
zation—"supervision," he writes, "is the worst aspect of
the penal system in Sakhalin"—and dreams of an integrated
community of educated people who will find meaning and

purpose and self-dignity in operating an enlightened colony.

The following chapter concerns the morality of the exiles—convicts and settlers—, whose "vices and perversions" are those of "people everywhere who are enslaved, hungry, and living in constant fear," and depicts also the punitive measures, including the floggings, that dehumanize, and make victims of, captor and captive alike. The spiritual paralysis, the death-in-life that had seemed T.'s alone before and during the early stages of his journey is here transferred to an entire suffering populace. Although he observed none of the capital punishments, he did talk to those who had, and quickly became aware of how the condemned prisoners' "fear of death" attached itself to the "free" residents, caught as they were in an unwholesome society and aware despite themselves of their complicity in the hangings. A priest told him that, after giving absolution as a young man to two convicts moments before they were escorted to the gallows, he "was afraid to enter a dark room for a long time"; and the chapter ends with a tale of mass hanging related to T. by a district commander of the southern region. Eleven men were to be hanged one after the other for murdering some members of a native tribe, but two cheated the executioner by poisoning themselves.

. . . An official read out the death sentence, trembling with nervousness and stuttering because he could not see well. The priest, dressed in black vestments, presented the Cross for all nine to kiss, and then turned to the district commander, whispering:

"For God's sake, let me go, I can't. . . ."

The procedure is a long one. Each man must be dressed in a shroud and led to the scaffold. When they finally hanged the nine men, they formed a garland in the air—these were the words of the district commander as he described the execution to me. When the bodies were taken down, the doctors found that one was still alive.

This incident had a peculiar significance. Everyone in the prison, all those who knew the innermost secrets of the crimes committed by the inmates—this included the hangman and his assistants—all of them knew the man still alive was innocent of the crime for which he was being hanged.

"They hanged him on another occasion," the district commander concluded his story. "Later, I could not sleep for a whole month."

By its placement as well as its subject, the penultimate chapter is the crucial one, and I would discuss it last. The concluding chapter, on diseases and medical treatment of the exiles, represents T.'s investigations as a doctor; but his interest is obviously in another kind of health. The records of sickness and death which he consulted for this chapter were hopelessly inadequate, as inadequate in their own way as the hospitals and clinics were for the treatment of patients. The ending trails off, and seems (like certain of his plays and stories) inconclusive; perhaps T. felt that his irony, which often escaped his literary critics, would elude the censors. The last page gives an inventory of the medical equipment, mostly broken, he found in the infirmaries, and of the medicines available as "cures" for the convicts' ailments; the last paragraph of the book cites, without comment, legislation that forbids convicts to engage in labor harmful to their health, even if they request it, as well as rules protecting the welfare of pregnant women and giving them lighter duties after delivery, during the period of breast-feeding.

As for the penultimate chapter, its subject is the very desire for freedom that sent T. on his own journey across Siberia. Given the brutalization and general malaise on this most imperfect of islands, it perhaps was inevitable that some of the more depraved criminals would take advantage of the wish for freedom on the part of others. Older convicts sometimes coaxed newcomers into attempting an escape, in order to murder them in the forests and swamps for the money they had brought with them, or simply to gain a reward of a few rubles for turning them over to the authorities. And yet the belief in the possibility of escape provided the only hope that a prisoner could have, and served, T. says, "as a kind of safety valve. If it were possible to deprive a convict of his hope of escaping as the only means to change his fate, to return from the dead, then . . . his despair would probably manifest itself in a more brutal and more horrible form than escaping."

Everything in this chapter gains its spiritual dimension from all the experiences that precede it. In first reading of the attempts at escape, I know that I was remembering not only the floggings, the fear of death, the miming of their illnesses by the prisoners on that rainy morning of T.'s deep despair, and the depiction of "domestic" life in the communal barracks, but the hardship of labor for the miners at Due and for convicts elsewhere on the island. Actually, the fettered miners at Due had a less arduous task than did those prisoners at Alexandrovsk who had been selected, on the basis of the soundness of their bodies as well as their previously-acquired skills, to be carpenters. They had the task not only of sawing and hammering, but of becoming beasts of burden, harnessed by chains to their logs, dragging them for miles from forest to town. A religious symbolism, however unconscious or unwilled, of necessity colors any description of carpenters undergoing such a burden. Its significance is such that T. returns to it in his final chapter; a few pages before his concluding paragraph on legislation forbidding labor detrimental to the health of the convicts, he refers to one doctor's opinion that the exertion required of men harnessed to heavy logs contributes to the high incidence of lung disease on the island.

Who would not dream of escaping such hardships,

such degradation? T. says that some prisoners vanish into the wilderness of the island's interior "to enjoy freedom for a month or a week; there are some who find even one day sufficient. The yearning for freedom seizes some people periodically and resembles drinking bouts and fits of epilepsy." One old convict at the southern post "takes a piece of bread, locks up his hut and, going no more than half a verst from the post, he sits on the side of the mountain and gazes at the taiga, the sea, and the sky. . . . There was a time when they used to beat him, but now they only laugh at his escapes."

The "unending awareness of life" as well as "the aspiration for freedom, which under normal circumstances is one of the most noble attributes of man," causes criminals to find "salvation in escape rather than in repentance and work," and were it "not for the fear of the physical difficulties of escaping," the island would be uninhabited. The prisoners "are able to see the mainland shore quite clearly even where the strait is at its widest. Every day the convict is fascinated and tempted by the hazy strip of shore with its lovely mountain peaks, which gives promise of freedom and the homeland," and some chance death from freezing, starving, and drowning in a desperate attempt to reach that far shore. Usually, those who survive the trip by raft or other means are recaptured on the mainland. The crimes for which a society normally punishes an offender—robbery, the selling of contraband merchandise, murder and lesser acts of violence—do not arouse in the authorities the fear they experience in confronting the desire for freedom, and do not generate such brutality of reprisal. The convicts of Sakhalin who are repeatedly recaptured on the mainland or while still drifting in the strait are the "incorrigible" criminals to be chained to iron balls or wheelbarrows, their bodies the ones most heavily scarred by the lash.

Somewhere in his letters, T. deplores the publication of his work in an ever-increasing number of foreign languages; he feels that his stories and plays, however accurate the translation, must remain unintelligible to persons not acquainted with the people and customs of his native land. For some years, I put off writing this account of his journey because I was both ignorant of his language and unacquainted with his culture. And yet I have not found my ignorance so much an impossible barrier as a means of illustrating how a strong voice can transcend a culture and even the very words it uses for expression. Even through the gauze of another language, a reader can hear T.'s voice, and sense how successful a given translation has been in carrying and sustaining it.

As a term in literary criticism, voice, which implies essence, has fallen into disfavor in our age, one which apparently has lost not only T.'s belief in the human future, but much of its faith in the integrity or constancy of personal identity and in the ability of words, translated or not, to communicate more than the relative truths—the conventional attitudes and clichés—of the sheltering or imprisoning culture. But the past is full of voices that escape confinement; and such voices, spiritual in nature, are the ones most of us who read still listen for. It is the voice of such a writer that I have heard in stories, and in the record of a journey—one suddenly decided upon, its motivation never clearly disclosed—to a penal colony. Out of my respect for his desire to be free, to escape social classification and all estimates of his worth as well as his own ego, I have called that writer only by initial throughout my account. Another writer who also desired liberation defines the nature of that voice as she attempts to explain the reason that in reading T.'s "little stories about nothing at all, the horizon widens; the soul gains an astonishing sense of freedom." Virginia Woolf says that he

> is aware of the evils and injustices of the social state; the condition of the peasants appals him, but the reformer's zeal is not his—that is not the signal for us to stop. The mind interests him enormously; he is a most subtle and delicate analyst of human relations. But

again, no; the end is not there. Is it that he is primarily
interested not in the soul's relation with other souls,
but with the soul's relation to health—with the soul's
relation to goodness? These stories are always showing us some affectation, pose, insincerity. Some
woman has got into a false relation; some man has
been perverted by the inhumanity of his circumstances. The soul is ill; the soul is cured; the soul is not
cured. Those are the emphatic points in his stories.

What, though, in that age of religious skepticism
which was hers as well as his and remains ours, is a "soul"?
What is its relationship, in a world without absolutes, to
"health" and "goodness"? Virginia Woolf does not say, but
her answer is implied in her reference to the sense of expanse and freedom experienced by the reader of his
stories—a response quite at odds with that of the characters
in them, paralyzed or imprisoned as they nearly always
are. Freedom is the soul's desire and identity, and were it
ever to be fully attained, the self would be extinguished and
the voice silent in that unity which, being beyond human
reason and consciousness, is Other and utterly indifferent
to us as separate creatures; health and goodness are known
by the degree to which we respect the potential for freedom in our fellows and do not pervert or thwart our own.
What is good reaches out toward sea, mountain, and
rarefied sky; what is bad or evil turns inward, poisoning
the mind and heart and lower viscera with its dark
secretions.

Although often described in other terms, such an
awareness is hardly original with T., and I had accepted it,
if on an abstract level, long before I carried to Florence a
paralysis of will, the affliction of a miserable and self-
centered despair, and a paperback collection of his stories.
What I hadn't known much about, until I began to read his
letters and biographies, was the extent of *his* despair, much
greater than mine despite his soul's knowledge, or the jour-

ney that was his soul's response to it. One flees death, according to legend, only to find Death waiting, as if by appointment, at the remote corner of the earth one has escaped to; but one can flee life as a loathsome prison to find it redeemed in an actual prison at the cold edge of the world. Halfway on his journey, T. found he wanted to live, immediately coloring other lives with his own elation and a rediscovered sense of the good. This was a necessary step; but only on the island, surrounded by what he recognized as idealistic illusion as well as actual evil, was he able to see at once human embodiments of the horror from which he had been in flight and the universality of his desire for freedom.

It is tempting to search T.'s book—God knows, I've done that more than once—for a particular encounter that could have provided him with a renewed or heightened awareness of his link with all mankind. Might it not have come as he was interviewing a convict baker, a person he admired—"a simple, openhearted and obviously good man," T. says of him—who managed not only to escape the island but to trudge across Siberia to his own village for a reunion with his wife and children before he was recaptured and sentenced to the inevitable flogging and longer term? Or might it not have come from his acquaintance with the "old convict woman" briefly assigned to him as a servant who found his personal possessions, including his blanket and the books she probably couldn't read, of extraordinary worth, for they recently had been in the country of her own dreaming? I doubt, though, that any single encounter had such a dramatic effect, for nearly all of the convicts he met equated a lost Russia with an ideal freedom, with the kind of happiness never to be found in any corner of the real world; and except for one—a sick and elderly man now securely fettered to his iron ball—all those he spoke with who had attempted the flight to freedom were glad they had chanced it, whatever their punishment.

"Things are boring here, your excellency. It is much better at home in Russia," T.'s convict driver said on that moonlit ride in the first or second week of his stay on the island. Four years before setting out for Sakhalin, in the period that preceded both his fame and his despair, T. wrote a little story about a nameless vagrant, an escaped convict who is being escorted by two soldiers to the authorities in the nearest town. The vagrant's hope is that he will be exiled to eastern Siberia, for in his imaginings not Russia but Siberia is the land of freedom. In eastern Siberia, the vagrant tells the soldiers, "everything's better"; the rivers contain more fish, exiles are given land and become both happy and prosperous. His fanciful descriptions of a bountiful and beautiful natural world, of immense plains and flowing waters, of dense tiers of evergreens rising from the riverbanks, give to the soldiers the belief that a life of freedom beyond their immediate experience truly exists. T. says that the images and visions that come to the soldiers as they slog with their skinny little captive through the mud and autumnal mists of the Russian countryside might have their source in "stories heard long ago" or be an inheritance from their "remote, free ancestors."

Sakhalin, then, gave to T. nothing he hadn't known all along. If the penal colony constituted a laboratory for his research, what it proved was the validity of his own intuitions, weakened by personal stress though they were. Perhaps despair—that absence of hope—is a requisite for any deepened understanding of a universal hope for something never to be found in the present time or place. How strange, and yet how inevitable, that the impulse toward a freedom beyond one's self and social identity would grant mutuality with all other individuals, however brutal and ignorant, giving significance to their very names, and would return one to the common world to struggle against its oppression and suffering while loving an evanescent life and its sensuous pleasures!

V

The Voyage Home

19

Spring comes early in Tuscany, and by mid-February, when the winter rains already had surrendered to a sun that blessed the snow-topped mountains I could see from my window, I was well into a novel I had not planned or consciously wanted to write. It was the story of man who, with his family, is caught up in racial animosities that resonate against an ugly and incomprehensible war. This man was not I—at least the details of our domestic and professional lives were different—but, in the manner of fiction, he did represent my soul's predicament. Liking others, he wants to be liked by them in turn; but slowly he becomes paralyzed by problems beyond any clear solution, losing a sustaining sense of the "good" in himself and in others. Surely he was I on the day I put him to bed in order to have him read T.'s letters, and gave him a transitory insight into the nature of T.'s journey. Like T., he too wanted freedom, escape.

The book was composed with a continuous excitement and haste new to me, but it took shape with no conscious plan or sense of outcome. At the end of each day I knew with absolute certainty—it always came as I washed the supper dishes, a task I insisted upon for the luck it brought—what I would write the following morning, but no more than that. Only on the day that I killed my protagonist in a chaotic scene of racial confrontation did I realize that the unconscious force impelling me each morning had been partly suicidal—that my impulse was to destroy a discredited social identity nearly fifty years in the making, a terrifying but necessary act if I were to liberate my soul for the purposes of life. I called the book *A Journey to Sahalin*, following the spelling of the island I found in the edition of T.'s letters I had been reading, a title that had more to do with the author than with his plot.

As for T. himself, my main character in the present drama, what remains to be said? He was glad to leave prison, but expunged its shadow only thousands of miles later on his homeward voyage, during a stopover on the tropical island he would remember for the remaining years of his life as a paradise. Here, in a "coconut grove on a moonlit night," he made love with his "black-eyed Hindu girl," and thus his experiences at the penal colony were framed before and after by that union in which the body momentarily achieves what is forever the soul's desire.

At another stopover, this time on the mainland, he bought what he took to be three mongooses, although the female turned out to be a palm civet, a fierce little creature that—after T. brought his three pets home—lurked under the furniture, darting out to fasten its teeth into the ankles of one guest or another. T.'s mother and brother Michael met him, much as they had left him, at a railroad station some distance from Moscow. They found him at a table in the station restaurant, surrounded by a crowd of fascinated onlookers, eating with two companions of his homeward journey and one mongoose. Although he provides no details, the biographer who gives the fullest account of T.'s life remarks that the reunion "of mother and son was a touching one."

T. did not, of course, live happily ever afterwards, even though his life on the estate and in the following years held fulfilling moments. In addition to helping build schools for peasant children and giving medical treatment to many people too poor to pay for it, he participated in another census—this time of all the inhabitants living in the vicinity of his estate—and in the exhausting preparations for an expected outbreak of cholera among them. He wrote many of his most glorious stories and plays. His last major story, one written about four years before his death, requires special mention. In it, a woman kills another's infant by pouring scalding laundry water over it in order to hold on to some real estate that the baby would have inherited. If the criminal is as depraved as any character in T.'s fiction, the grieving mother is his most forgiving and compassionate human construction; and although the story depicts humanity at its worst—there are other crimes as well—it ends with a sense of blessedness. The most religious of all his creative works in its depiction of good and evil and its final transcendence of the dark valley of its setting, this story came from the insight into peasant character that T.'s years of country living gave him; and yet—as his brother Michael said—it depended at least as much upon what he had discovered at Sakhalin.

A gradual cooling of his friendship with Suvorin, combined with the urging of Tolstoy, led T. to choose another publisher, one who would print an inexpensive edition of his collected works, and his new contract was not in his best interests. Still, the income from his writing was sufficient for one who had not long to live. Among the contributions his means enabled him to make was an anonymous gift of money to his old friend Olga Kundasov, whose existence had become precarious. He married an actress he loved, although the advanced state of his illness, as well as that continued yearning for an impossible freedom, made him reluctant: having given in at last to the entreaties of his beloved, he journeyed from Yalta to Moscow for the ceremony, but left the necessary documents behind, thus managing a temporary postponement.

On his homeward voyage from the island, a typhoon so nearly caused the ship to founder—it heeled in the gusts at a thirty-eight-degree angle—that the captain advised him to have his pistol ready, for suicide was preferable to death by water; this counterpart to the frightening collision with the three mail carts produced no psychic illumination, for T. now simply wanted to live. Two passengers died aboard ship, and their bodies, after a brief ceremony, were given in their canvas shrouds to the sea. The typhoon and dual burial came before paradise triumphed over the long prison shadow; afterwards, as the ship continued through the calm and tropical seas, T. repeated several times the act that once terrified Mary: jumping off the deck to grab a rope thrown by a sailor at the stern. On one such occasion, he saw nearby a shark accompanied by its school of pilot fish. In this flouting of death there lies a fourth simulation of the outward journey: we recall that T., as he coerced his driver onto a flooded plain from which there could be no turning back, was remembering the "incomprehensible impulse of defiance," that ardor for life, expressed in an earlier dive from a deck.

Perhaps the return from any long and strenuous spiritual journey contains this curious mirroring of the outward trek, a dream-like effect that prepares the sojourner for his habitual life by assuring him that the reality he found was only illusion. Perhaps it is an actual requirement for his physical and emotional safety, much as the deliberate stages of a deep-sea diver's bubbling ascent from the ocean floor are required if he is to adjust to the conventional atmospheric pressure. In any event, before the ship reached its destined harbor, T. had completed a story in which certain of his homeward experiences are transformed by the larger experience of the whole journey. I take it as a record of what he had learned, set down before daily living could obscure it. If it, like so many other of his stories, uses competing aspects of his nature to define its characters, it more than any other reveals his spiritual essence—the degree of his insight into the goal of that desire for freedom which for him underlies all of our values.

Both of the two major characters are dying, aboard the ship returning them from the East. One is a simple and uneducated peasant, a discharged army orderly so accepting of, or oblivious to, distinctions and divisions that were it not for his singular and unreasoning hatred of all Chinese, a reader would be hard put to define him. In the hallucinations of his approaching death, he is intermittently oppressed by the nightmare of the eyeless bull's head and released from it by dreams of homeland and snow— the homeland becoming, as it does for the convicts of Sakhalin, for T. himself, and for so many others, past and present, in exile from Russia, a place and condition of spiritual freedom wholly distinct from political or national considerations.

The other character, an intellectual and a malcontent, is aware of nothing but distinctions and differentiations, of political oppression and social injustice. His esteem for his own acumen gives him hubris, a belief in his power over natural processes and a sense of his superiority to such a stupid peasant as his dying companion. If the peasant approximates the human soul both in his longing for home and in his effortless acceptance of nearly everything in the natural as well as the social world, the intellectual represents the separate self—a consciousness that, unchecked by anything beyond its egocentric apprehension of the material realm, infects the body with bitterness and leads to alienation. The intellectual's life is the first to be extinguished. The story gains its title from the peasant's name, Gusev, and it is his death, presented so laconically one is hardly aware of it, and his burial by water that conclude it.

I have always been struck by the intentional intrusion of the pathetic fallacy upon the terrifying detachment of the final section of this story. Chekhov—why not call him that, now that I am freed of him and he of my meddling?— uses that fallacy as a last means of attempting to enforce a human meaning on a fusion of water and sky, of substance and spirit, a unity so indifferent to, and separate from, consciousness that words are incapable of expressing its beauty, even though the soul acknowledges it as its homeland:

20

Gusev goes back to the infirmary and gets into his bunk. He is again tormented by a vague desire and he can't make out what it is that he wants. There is a weight on his chest, a throbbing in his head, his mouth is so dry that it is difficult for him to move his tongue. He dozes and talks in his sleep and, worn out with nightmares, with coughing and the stifling heat, towards morning he falls into a heavy sleep. He dreams that they have just taken the bread out of the oven in the barracks and that he has climbed into the oven and is having a steam bath there, lashing himself with a besom of birch twigs. He sleeps for two days and on the third at noon two sailors come down and carry him out of the infirmary. He is sewn up in sailcloth and to make him heavier, they put two gridirons in with him. Sewn up in sailcloth, he looks like a carrot or a radish: broad at the head and narrow at the feet. Before sunset, they carry him on deck and put him on a plank. One end of the plank lies on the ship's rail, the other on a box placed on a stool. Round him stand the discharged soldiers and the crew with heads bared.

"Blessed is our God," the priest begins, "now, and ever, and unto ages of ages."

"Amen," three sailors chant.

The discharged men and the crew cross themselves and look off at the waves. It is strange that a man should be sewn up in sailcloth and should soon be flying into the sea. Is it possible that such a thing can happen to anyone?

The priest strews earth upon Gusev and makes obeisance to him. The men sing "Memory Eternal."

The seaman on watch duty raises the end of the plank, Gusev slides off it slowly and then flying, head foremost, turns over in the air and—plop! Foam covers him, and for a moment he seems to be wrapped in lace, but the instant passes and he disappears in the waves.

He plunges rapidly downward. Will he reach the bottom? At this spot the ocean is said to be three miles deep. After sinking sixty or seventy feet, he begins to descend more and more slowly, swaying rhythmically as though in hesitation, and, carried along by the current, moves faster laterally than vertically.

And now he runs into a school of fish called pilot fish. Seeing the dark body, the little fish stop as though petrified and suddenly all turn round together and disappear. In less than a minute they rush back at Gusev, swift as arrows, and begin zigzagging round him in the water. Then another dark body appears. It is a shark. With dignity and reluctance, seeming not to notice Gusev, as it were, it swims under him; then while he, moving downward, sinks upon its back, the shark turns, belly upward, basks in the warm transparent water and languidly opens its jaws with two rows of teeth. The pilot fish are in ecstasy; they stop to see what will happen next. After playing a little with the body, the shark nonchalantly puts his jaws under it, cautiously touches it with his teeth and the sailcloth is ripped the full length of the body, from head to foot; one of the gridirons falls out, frightens the pilot fish and, striking the shark on the flank, sinks rapidly to the bottom.

Meanwhile, up above, in that part of the sky where the sun is about to set, clouds are massing, one resembling a triumphal arch, another a lion, a third a pair of scissors. A broad shaft of green light issues from the clouds and reaches to the middle of the sky; a while later, a violet beam appears alongside of it and then a golden one and a pink one . . . The heavens turn a soft lilac tint. Looking at this magnificent enchanting sky, the ocean frowns at first, but soon it, too, takes on tender, joyous, passionate colors for which it is hard to find a name in the language of man.

—SECTION V OF "Gusev,"
TRANSLATED BY AVRAHM YARMOLINSKY

Acknowledgments
and Notes

My greatest indebtedness is to the translators of the two books that influenced me during my year in Florence: *Letters of Anton Tchehov to His Family and Friends*, with biographical sketch, translated by Constance Garnett, published in 1920 by Chatto & Windus, a book not quite identical with the American edition published by Macmillan the same year and which I will be using for the following references; and *The Portable Chekhov*, edited and largely translated by Avrahm Yarmolinsky, published in 1947 by Viking Press. The translation of the final section of "Gusev" with which I end my book comes from *The Portable Chekhov;* the general value of that collection to me both in Florence and while reconstructing Chekhov's journey is perhaps made evident in my text. I also owe special gratitude to Simon Karlinsky, who, for the sake of accuracy in a subject that matters deeply to him, agreed to read the manuscript for factual errors and mistranslations of the major quotations; any remaining errors are a result of my own perversity or ignorance, and the interpretations of facts and translations are, of course, wholly my own.

Beyond such personal indebtedness, I owe much to all those who provided the documentary evidence that enabled me to tell the story of a spiritual quest. For biographical information, I have depended upon *Chekhov: A Biography* by Ernest J. Simmons, published in 1962 by

Little, Brown, and reissued as a paperback by the University of Chicago Press in 1970; and *A New Life of Anton Chekhov* by Ronald Hingley, published by Alfred A. Knopf in 1976. The latter work is more rigorous in its exclusion of dubious material than the former, but the degree and intimacy of detail in the earlier biography made it at least as valuable to me. My chapters on Sakhalin would have been guesswork without the substance provided by Chekhov's *The Island: A Journey to Sakhalin,* translated by Luba and Michael Terpak, published in 1967 by Washington Square Press and reprinted in 1977 by Greenwood Press.

The Garnett translation of the letters contains a more generous portion of Chekhov's correspondence during the Sakhalin journey than do either of the two latest translations of the letters, both entitled *Letters of Anton Chekhov* and both published in 1973, one of them selected and edited by Avrahm Yarmolinsky and published by Viking Press, the other translated by Michael Henry Heim in collaboration with Simon Karlinsky and published by Harper & Row. Still, I have found both of these collections useful for other letters; and the introduction, commentary, and notes that Karlinsky provides in his volume are of exceptional merit.

As a long-time reader of Chekhov's fiction, I have consciously and no doubt unconsciously absorbed all the translations that have come my way, from those of Marian Fell published in 1915 to the latest of Ronald Hingley's contributions in the Oxford Chekhov series; but I should here express a special indebtedness to Ann Dunnigan for her translation of "In Exile," included among her other translations in *Anton Chekhov: Selected Stories,* published in 1960 by New American Library.

I am grateful that I have been allowed to rummage among the works of these and other scholars and translators. While far from complete, the following notes indicate the sources of my major borrowings and give as well the sources for the facts or events that underlie those dramatic scenes which obviously are of my invention:

CHAPTER 1

p. 3 "... might have been nearing a breakdown ..." See Hingley, p. 130, and "Unsolved Problems," pp. 119–26; and Simmons, "There Is a Sort of Stagnation in My Soul," pp. 174–204.

p. 10 For the letter to Suvorin, see Garnett, pp. 119–20.

CHAPTER 2

p. 12 For a description of the house on Sadovaya-Kudrinskaya Street, see Simmons, p. 108.

pp. 13–21 The letter-writing scene is of course imagined; for this letter, I have used the Heim-Karlinsky translation, pp. 158–61.

p. 19 The American critic is Irving Howe; the writer he is addressing, Ralph Ellison. My quotation comes from Karlinsky's commentary; see Heim and Karlinsky, p. 152.

CHAPTER 3

p. 21 The abridged version of Michael's memoir in Garnett does not provide this "moment of decision"; my source for it is Simmons, p. 204.

p. 23 "We just looked closely into each other's eyes ..." This prose must be blamed on Lydia Avilova, author of *Chekhov in My Life;* my quotation comes from Hingley, p. 197.

p. 24 "... suicidal tendency ..." Though normally he finds Chekhov anything but a melancholy and depressed person, Ivan Bunin advances this as a factor in both the marriage and the trip; see Hingley, p. 278 and p. 285.

p. 24 The "bitter letter" is to Vukol Lavrov; see Heim and Karlinsky, pp. 165–67.

CHAPTER 4

For the names of the people who accompanied Chekhov on the train to Yaroslavl, see Simmons, p. 217. Although the scenes on the train are inventions, the characterizations are based on what I have learned about these people in the biographies and elsewhere, including (for Isaac Levitan and the Kuvshinnikovs) Chekhov himself. His story "The Butterfly" provides an example of how even the most generous-spirited of writers can lose friendships by modeling his characters on actual people.

p. 27   ". . . the first name of the compliant Dr. Kuvshinnikov . . ." A kindly man deserves to have his first name mentioned, if only in a footnote. According to Karlinsky, that name is Dmitry.

CHAPTER 5

p. 37   For Paul's behavior in Moscow, including his posting of the "schedule of duties for the children," see Simmons, pp. 28–29, and Hingley, pp. 20–21.

p. 39   For the labors of Chekhov and his family at their new estate, see Simmons, pp. 269–72, and Hingley, pp. 160–62.

pp. 42–45   The story referred to is "Gooseberries"; the passages quoted are from the translation of it in *The Portable Chekhov*, pp. 371–84.

CHAPTER 6

Olga Kundasov did accompany Chekhov for a few days on the river; his unease in writing of this fact to his family perhaps helps to explain the description of her in the letter (Garnett, p. 144) quoted at the end of this chapter. I have loosely based my characterization of Olga on this and other letters, as well as on what Karlinsky and the biographers indicate about her nature, although I have not included in my depiction the self-righteous or dogmatic aspect of her radicalism that often made her an irritant to others. In "Three Years," Chekhov apparently modeled the music teacher Polina Rassudina on Olga; the irritating qualities are evident in the portrayal. Karlinsky says that Chekhov and Olga's "period of greatest closeness seems to have been just prior to his departure for Sakhalin" (Heim and Karlinsky, p. 197), a conjecture of obvious appeal to me. The work of "T.'s" fiction over which I have her musing is "A Dreary Story." The quotation about learning (p. 50) comes from the translation of that story by Ronald Hingley in *Chekhov: Seven Stories*, published by Oxford University Press; see pp. 101–102.

The scenes aboard ship, including the nightmare, also are imaginative renderings. Chekhov gives the image of the eyeless bull's head to Gusev, in the story of that title; intuitively, I have always attributed the power of that image—in his introduction (p. xxxvi) to *The Island*, Robert Payne refers to it as "the ultimate horror, the symbol of all that was powerful, degrading and meaningless in life"—to the intensity of Chekhov's own dreams, although I have no evidence for that other than its affinity with the actual nightmare which gave him the seed of "The Black Monk." On a literal level, the black bull's head in "Gusev" could be, I suppose, the afterimage on the character's retina caused by his peering at the cabin porthole of his ship; but such neurological effects gain their interpretations in the mind—in the case of this story, the minds of author and reader, since simple Gusev experiences neither "horror" nor the angst of "meaninglessness." The eyeless bull's head represents for me—and has, ever since I read the story in Florence—all the diverse accounts of despair in Chekhov, referring to blindness as they frequently do, and has connections with his surreal sense during the early portions of the trip of people as jutting-browed giants and jackdaws with great heads; and I assume it has its source in his subconscious processes. My use of that image in advance of the composition of the story remains, however, a deviation from known "fact." Enough! If I carry this footnote any further, I will be as suspect as any composer of such notes in the fiction of Vladimir Nabokov.

CHAPTER 9

p. 78   The story referred to is "The Steppe."

p. 81   The long letter to Mary that contains not only this description of the accident but a greal deal of the other material in this and later chapters is to be found in Garnett, pp. 159–74. The letters preceding and following it are also of exceptional interest.

CHAPTER 10

The opening scene in the post house is my invention, though one based on information found in the letters.

pp. 92–95   The story is "In Exile."

p. 95   ". . . having brought to his mind a mysterious pool . . ." In his long letter to Mary, Chekhov remarks, "Before going to sleep I wrote a letter to Marya Vladimirovna; I was reminded of the Bozharovsky pool." See Garnett, p. 168. I refer to Mary Kiselyov [Marya Vladimirovna] as "gay and imprudent" because her general attitudes, like those of Lyubov Ranevskaya in *The Cherry Orchard*, helped to bring her estate to ruin.

CHAPTER 12

p. 105   The petition to the state administrator of prisons is translated in Heim and Karlinsky, pp. 154–55.

p. 106   "From the details he gives in the letter . . .": The letter to Suvorin upon which I base nearly all of my scene with the assistant chief of police of Tomsk is found in Garnett, pp. 176–81; for the small addition about the tour of the whorehouses, see Yarmolinsky, p. 154.

p. 108   "An Attack of Nerves" is the title of the story

about the students' visit to the brothels; see *The Portable Chekhov*, pp. 222–51.

CHAPTER 13

p. 114   For the letter to Leykin, see Garnett, pp. 186–88 Other letters on which the material of this chapter is based will be found in Garnett, pp. 181–213.

p. 122   For the reference to the affair with the Japanese girl in Blagoveshchensk, see Heim and Karlinsky, p. 168. The original censor of this material was not a bureaucrat, but Chekhov's sister. Soviet censors, though, cut out even the sentence about the Japanese girl's room that Mary had permitted to remain in her edition of the letters. See Heim and Karlinsky, pp. 169–70.

CHAPTER 15

p. 136   The story referred to is "The Black Monk." For my quotation from it, I am indebted to *Anton Chekhov: Selected Stories*, translated by Jessie Coulson, Oxford University Press; see p. 73. Note: All but one of the quotations about Sakhalin, which begin in this chapter and continue into Chapter 18, have their origin in the Terpak translation of *The Island*, although Karlinsky has corrected and otherwise improved much of what I have used. The exception is the quoted dialogue with the boy, given on p. 155; here I have followed Heim and Karlinsky, pp. 179–80. Page numbers of my text precede the subject matter, given in parentheses, and are followed by the page numbers of the sources in *The Island*.

CHAPTER 16

pp. 143–44   (dinner party conversation), pp. 21–22; p. 146 (passage dictated by Baron Korf), p. 27; p. 147 (footnote about General Kononovich), pp. 339–40.

p. 149 (first quoted passage), pp. 27–28; pp. 149–50 (second quoted passage), pp. 28–29.

CHAPTER 17

p. 154   (statistics about children), p. 255; p. 156 (quoted footnote), pp. 262–64; p. 158 (encounter with sick man at Due), p. 111; (profiteering by private corporation), pp. 104–106; p. 159 (encounter with Gilyaks), pp. 150–51; pp. 160–61 (mistreatment of women), pp. 231–44; p. 161 (communal wards), pp. 100–102; pp. 162–63 (the flogging), pp. 330–32.

CHAPTER 18

pp. 164–66 (description of settlement and account of night in warehouse), pp. 122–25; p. 167 (the Pacific Ocean), p. 188; p. 169 (the mass hangings), p. 335; pp. 170–172 (references to freedom and attempted escapes), pp. 341–55.

p. 173   Virginia Woolf's comments about Chekhov are from her essay "The Russian Point of View" in *The Common Reader*, first series. The quotation will be found on p. 181 of the Harvest edition, published by Harcourt Brace Jovanovich.

p. 176   The story is "Daydreams"; a translation will be found in *The Portable Chekhov*, pp. 108–18.

CHAPTERS 19 and 20

p. 181   The story referred to is "In the Ravine"; a translation will be found in *The Portable Chekhov*, pp. 461–512.

p. 183   As indicated, the story is "Gusev." The quotation from it comes from *The Portable Chekhov*, pp. 266–68.

James McConkey's *Court of Memory* is also available in an Obelisk edition.